Advance praise for *Discover Your Soul Potential*

"*Discover Your Soul Potential* is a fresh and coherent new presentation of the Enneagram that makes it easy to understand why the types function as they do. In also developing the concept of repressed center, it offers a sensible and practical approach to transformation."

— **GERALD MAY**, author
Will and Spirit and *Addiction and Grace*

"The Enneagram is coming to spiritual maturity in this book. Hurley and Donson show an amazing level of insight and experience with the genius of the Enneagram."

— **RICHARD ROHR, O.F.M.**, co-author,
Discovering the Enneagram and *Everything Belongs*

"A wonderful way to understand our souls' desire."

— **DENIE HIESTAND**, dean,
International Academy of Vibrational Medical Science,
author of *Electrical Nutrition* and *Journey to Truth*

"The depth of Kathy and Theodorre's understanding of human nature and spirituality is rare in the materialistic outlook of the present day. Their beliefs shine through every page of *Discover Your Soul Potential*. This is a book to use and to live by."

— **RAY KEEDY-LILLEY, M.A.N.L.P.**,
director of the National School of Hypnosis and
Psychotherapy, London, England

"Hurley and Donson's teaching of the Enneagram is a highly effective, inspiring and positive approach that greatly reduces the time and effort needed to come to an in-depth understanding of the essential elements of each personality type. This book unfolds each type in a clear, logical, and easily assimilated manner."

— PAUL BONHAM, past president,
International Enneagram Association

"Kathy and Theodorre's innovative model of the Ennea-gram has transformed and enriched the lives of those who have studied with them. This book will allow their wisdom to reach the wider audience it demands."

— ROBERT SIUDZINSKI, PH. D., professor,
University of North Florida

"Readers will refer again and again to this small but mighty volume, which is an uncomplicated but greatly expanded Enneagram guide for attaining a deep understanding of who we are, and who we could be. The possibilities it offers for soul growth are stunning."

— BETSY CARR MCGEE, senior consultant,
The McGee Group, Inc.

DEDICATION

This book is dedicated to the Source of all Wisdom

And to all of our students

And companions on the soul quest

Who asked the penetrating questions

That caused us to search beneath the surface

And discover the insights that resulted in this book.

May we continue to learn from one another.

Other Books by Kathy Hurley and Theodorre Donson

What's My Type?
Use the Enneagram System of Nine Personality Types
to Discover Your Best Self

My Best Self:
Using the Enneagram to Free the Soul

Discover Your Soul Potential

Using the Enneagram
To Awaken Spiritual Vitality

Kathy Hurley
and
Theodorre Donson

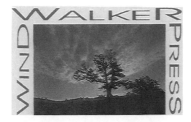

ACKNOWLEDGMENTS

First and foremost, we gratefully acknowledge the life and teaching of Dr. Maurice Nicoll (1884 - 1953), whose ideas and principles underpin this entire book. Although he may be little known, we consider him to be the towering spiritual figure of the twentieth century and his books to be a worthy pursuit for anyone who wants to awaken soul.

We are deeply grateful to Erin Kemp, our daughter and assistant, whose dedication and consummate skills have been invaluable in the writing and production of this book. We are equally grateful to her husband, Todd, for his love and support, and to their son, Walker, who is the third generation to benefit from the guidance of this wisdom.

Special thanks go to our Enneagram study group — especially to its original members, Joni Seivert, Sam Shone, Wendy Williams and Jack Zordan — for supporting us personally and helping us refine our ideas.

This book would not exist were it not for the enthusiasm, expertise and guidance of Christine Testolini, our self-publishing consultant; her support and tireless effort went far beyond the call of professional duty. We are also grateful to everyone who had to work under the duress of publication deadlines: Barbara McNichol for her expertise in copyediting; Ann Marie Gordon for her invaluable assistance in the production of this book; Li Hertzi for her superb cover design; and Lynda Stannard who indexed the book.

CONTENTS

INTRODUCTION

JOURNEY INTO SOUL

"Everyone is free to change. Most people just don't believe it."

— Anthony de Mello

Discover Your Soul Potential is a synthesis of the past 30 years that each of us, both personally and professionally, have devoted to learning, understanding and applying the spiritual wisdoms that lead to the development of soul. While our search has led each of us, individually and together, down inspiring and sometimes diverse paths, one point has become amazingly clear to us: authentic spirituality and transformation are born out of simple ideas, not complicated ones.

Complexity overstimulates our intellectualized western minds. With the mind racing — even with inspiring ideas and insights — we think and talk about transformation without actually experiencing it. We live in the illusion that *thinking and talking* about transformation is the same as *living* it.

We have come to believe that grounded spirituality rises out of simple, practical, everyday values such as human kindness, service, compassion and gratitude. These values that make life meaningful. In the words of the Dalai Lama,

1

"The education of the heart is vital. We must have a sense of caring for one another because the destruction of your enemy is destruction of yourself. Our way of life is so interconnected."

Through the years we have studied a wide variety of spiritual disciplines, psychologies and theologies. We have been spellbound by the soul-stirring creativity, insight and wisdom that has leapt off the pages of books written by both ancient and modern spiritual seekers. We have also been amazed by the power of grace and insight in our own spiritual experiences as we have applied this wisdom to our lives.

Growing Our Souls

Looking back we realize that, since our childhoods, both of us have been yearning to develop our souls. Though not an inevitability (for soul development is always a choice), growing our own souls seems, from the vantage point of today, to be the purpose and the passion of our lives.

For some readers, the idea of "growing our souls" may seem foreign, as it did to us when we first heard the phrase. Both of us grew up in traditional Catholic families and parishes where we learned the traditional ideas about soul. These notions said we are created with a soul fully intact, that at birth our souls were afflicted with the defect of "original sin" from which God and the church saved us through baptism. We learned that our life responsibility is to preserve our souls from personal sin by obeying the laws of God and the church.

The spiritual practices of the church (for Catholics, those would include the sacraments, such as confession and holy communion, and other devotional practices) would sanctify our souls so we could remain close to God and go to heaven after we die. Although the details may differ widely, every religion we are aware of proposes a similar paradigm to its members for finding its version of what institutional Christianity calls "salvation."

This paradigm has merit at certain stages of spiritual development. Yet there comes a time when a person on a spiritual search outgrows that paradigm and needs a new model, a new vision of both the challenge and the process of personal spiritual growth.

We and many others have found that new model we seek in the paradigm of "growing our souls." This model doesn't invalidate the model described above. Rather, it envelopes and builds upon the inner discipline it promotes, and then it frees a person's soul to take the next steps toward personal transformation.

In this model we realize that, while soul is real, its strength lies in its potential. If it is to grow, we must accept the responsibility to develop it. If our souls remain undeveloped and insubstantial, we do not have the spiritual force to protect us from automatically reacting to the cares and anxieties of life.

We develop "soul strength" by questioning, searching and acting on our dissatisfaction with being ignorant. Pursuing art, personalizing morality, and searching for meaning in life's experiences also develop soul. Questioning our values, freeing expression of the body in games and movement, and developing inner discipline further strengthen soul. This partial list gives us a taste for both the struggle and fulfillment that growing our souls involves.

The Body Lives in the Soul

Our search to grow our own souls has led us to a second untraditional belief about the soul. If you questioned most people on the idea, they probably would say that the soul lives in the body. We have come to believe the reverse: *that the body lives in the soul.*

The soul is, to use a metaphor, an energy field around the body. Whether your energy field is strong or weak is up to your development of it. In past centuries, this energy field around people who had grown their own souls was interpreted as a "halo." Today people call it an "aura." Some people claim to see and read auras to identify the nature and the relative state of health of the soul.

The belief that the body lives in the soul helps us understand why people react the way they do to the pressures, cares, anxieties and experiences of life. People in whom soul energy is weak react directly to all of life's experiences. Surely, people can live in the world this way. Their soul has little energy, and so it is a thin layer through which daily life easily penetrates. Living in their outer personality only (the identifications, defense mechanisms, reactions and skills we

4

name the "ego"), these people learn to get by, get along and get ahead, or they can learn the reverse. But most importantly, they live their lives as if this is all life was meant to be. Playing life's victims or victors, they learn little from their experiences because their weak souls are wedded to the world of constant cares. That's where they devote all their energy.

However, when people develop soul strength, the experiences of life must first pass through and be interpreted by soul and its values. The stronger the soul or true self, the more depth, purpose and direction their lives have because the soul adds new dimensions of meaning to each experience. These are the people who make a more insightful comment, a greater contribution, a more constructive response to the problems, issues and experiences of daily life.

Kathy's Story

I am a cradle Catholic, the fifth of seven children who was raised in the house my paternal grandfather built in a small town in northern Minnesota. At the age of six months, I developed whooping cough, which was immediately followed by a series of childhood illnesses. Until I was four, I spent as much time in the hospital as I did at home, and even at home a nurse was often needed to care for me full time.

During a blizzard, I had to be given a blood transfusion on the dining room table. My dad was the donor, and fortunately our blood was a match since there were no facilities to test our compatibility beforehand. I received the last rites of the church once, and twice I spent two weeks in an oxygen tent.

Over 50 years after the fact, my admiration for the love that I knew my parents had to have during those difficult years of my illness soared to new heights. I learned the doctors told my parents that, although my survival depended on receiving oxygen, the inevitable result would be that I would be blind, deaf, mentally retarded or all three. (In fact, it was only about 15 to 20 years ago that the medical profession learned how to regulate the oxygen dosage for a baby so that this kind of damage would no longer occur.) Their fear of killing or physically injuring their child through these medical procedures must have been overwhelming but were faced with an even greater courage.

Therefore, in my early grade school years, I decided that God must have something special for me to do or I wouldn't have survived as a healthy child. However, that idea slowly slipped from consciousness as I grew up and began living an ordinary life. I attended a Catholic grade school, a public high school and a Catholic college. Then I married, had three children and never wanted to be anything more than I was — a full-time mom.

Throughout my life, I faithfully practiced my religion and taught my children to do the same. It never occurred to me to question anything. Blind as that kind of faith may seem, the inner discipline developed by regular practices such as attending weekly and sometimes daily mass, keeping holy the Sabbath, not eating meat on Fridays, and fasting on the proscribed days gave me an inner strength and grounding for a time yet to come.

In 1969, a friend called and wanted to talk about a problem she was having. She was pregnant and, due to a series of complications, her doctor told her there was a 90% chance her child would suffer from severe physical and mental handicaps. He recommended she have an abortion. Because of our conversations during the next few days, my friend decided against the abortion.

Her courage and my exaggerated sense of responsibility for the welfare of this baby drove me to my knees for the next seven months. I had always believed that miracles would happen when they were needed. I felt confident that, more than anything, God would want to heal an innocent baby if someone would just ask. That was my job and I took it seriously.

In early spring, my friend's beautiful, perfectly formed baby was born and died shortly afterwards due to internal medical complications. I felt that my faith died with this baby. It was replaced by a raging anger towards God — if, in truth, there even was a God.

Little did I know that night over 30 years ago that, as I stood shaking my fists at the heavens and screaming at God, my prayers for a healthy new life were being answered in ways far greater than I could have ever asked or imagined.

Six weeks after the death of her child, my friend again became pregnant. Even though her doctor told her the chances of her having a deformed child were slightly higher than before, she never considered having an abortion. So here I was, back on my knees. This time, she gave birth to a healthy child who has grown into a beautiful human being inside and out.

So the miracle did happen! Not only to the baby but also to me. As I continued to wrestle with God, a lifetime of illusions about who God is, who I am and what faith, hope, love and prayer are all began to dissolve. Slowly, the unasked questions of a lifetime began to tumble forth. My need to understand propelled me on a journey that would forever change my life.

In the 1970s, my learning and unlearning curve spiraled upwards. I took courses in scripture, the Desert Fathers and Mothers, church history, Christian formation, healing prayer, contemplative prayer, Jungian psychology and dream interpretation. I joined a prayer group, learned to play the guitar, led the music ministry, learned to paint and led retreats. I was even chosen to lead a prayer group that had grown to several hundred members in a generally "no women in leadership allowed" organization. Life was an exciting, wonderful adventure!

The 1980s ushered in a new life cycle, one that would prove to deepen and stabilize the lessons I had learned in the 1970s.

Theodorre's Story

I was born in an orphanage run by Catholic Charities of the Chicago archdiocese. Five weeks later, I was adopted by my parents as their first child. They had been on the adoption waiting list for only a short while but sped to the head of the list due to the influence of my father's uncle, a priest highly placed in the Vatican and an advisor to the then-current pope. Almost three years later, my parents adopted a little girl.

From the outside, our family looked like a normal, middle class, urban family headed by hard-working people who had grown up during the Great Depression and knew the value of a dollar. Like many in their generation, my parents strived to get ahead so they could give to their children more than they had been given.

However, on the inside, our family was fraught with disruptive psychological and spiritual energies. Actions were driven by much pain that had never been resolved for several generations in both my parents' family trees. My mother especially bore dramatic scars from her childhood experience and only found peace with herself in the last years of her life. Add to that the sadness and pain my sister and I brought to the mix as children given away by their birth parents. Home life felt very unsafe and insecure to this little boy.

So I withdrew into the world of books, music, art and religion. These four influences became the hallmarks of my childhood, and I spent most of my time in these pursuits. They were safe because the sisters who staffed our Catholic school and the priests who staffed our parish were, if a little emotionally remote, kind and intelligent people who genuinely loved and competently educated and protected the children placed in their care.

As I look back, I realize that wonderful spiritual experiences of communion with God marked my childhood. The divine archetypes entered my life on a regular basis to provide the nurturing that my psychological environment could not. However, not being able to discuss these experiences with anyone, I could not fully appropriate the love I was receiving. Consequently, childhood mostly felt like a forlorn desert.

As I reached puberty, I decided I was incapable of loving others. (As I look back, I see this as one of those wrong conclusions that children often make because they do not have enough accurate information with which to interpret their experiences.) High school was a time of academic achievement, a flurry of extracurricular activities and social development.

By the time I entered seminary at the college level to become a Catholic priest, I had decided that, since I was incapable of love, the goal of my service to others would be to completely understand the most complicated ideas. Then I would be able to explain them in the simplest of terms so the average person could understand them. Now I realize that, while in my early years I had developed the art of self-expression in several fields, this definition of my life purpose indicated the degree to which I had given up the hope of ever being personally happy.

However, just before my ordination, something happened that began to unravel the pain of my past and open me to new possibilities. I met a woman who prayed with me for the healing of my inner child. It was a guided visual meditation in which painful childhood experiences were reframed with God's love for me surrounding them. Because one of my responses to being adopted was always feeling alienated from others, this prayer was a profound experience of freedom, joy and grace. It seemed as if veils fell from my eyes. I was able to see myself and life from a much more positive point of view.

This was the first of many steps. As a way of dealing with the many wounds from my childhood, I entered "healing of memories" sessions regularly for several years. Because I found these sessions helpful, after my ordination to the priesthood I began conducting them myself both with individuals and with groups. I also grounded my spiritual work in the psychology of Carl Jung.

I wrote two books on inner healing (under the name "Theodore E. Dobson," which was my name until, for both personal and professional reasons, I legally took the name "Theodorre Donson" in August 1998). From 1978 to 1989, I traveled around North America presenting retreats and other programs about inner healing.

During the first years of ministry, I also carried out the responsibilities of a parish priest. These included the call to serve the sick and bereaved, to love and minister to people some of whom I personally disagreed with or didn't like, to keep a daily schedule of responsibilities to parish organizations and individuals, and to continue the intellectual work of developing my understanding of psychology and theology.

Fulfilling these roles created an inner discipline that grounded my explorations into the unknown world of soul development. Having resigned from the Catholic priesthood in spring of 1990 (and later having been officially released from my priestly vows), I continue to be grateful for the opportunities for service created in that role. In so many ways, it prepared me for the work I do today.

Two Journeys Converge

In 1978, Kathy was organizing a healing service for the Denver Metro area and she invited Theodorre to be the celebrant. Then, three years later, Theodorre was invited by Denver's archbishop to create a spirituality resource center for the Denver archdiocese. He invited Kathy to work with him on the project.

In this context, we discovered the Enneagram. Through years of experience, we had come to believe in the reality of spiritual healing. We could point to many cases, including our own, to authenticate its reality. However, we also knew people who seemed to reach a certain point in the healing process and then stop. Through spiritual direction and healing prayer activities, we would see people deal with an issue and think it was resolved, only to find them returning a few months later with the same difficulty.

Then, in her role as co-director of the center, Kathy attended a conference on contemplative prayer. As a way of getting to know her assigned roommate, she and the other woman began to share some of their recent experiences.

The other woman shared, "Last weekend I attended an Enneagram workshop."

Kathy replied, "What's an Enneagram?"

The woman responded, "Oh, you wouldn't like it. I just hated it."

Kathy said, "Well then tell me something about it so I can avoid it if I come across it."

But as the woman described her negative experience of the Enneagram, everything inside Kathy responded positively. Something rose up in Kathy to say, "If anything here is true, this is what we've been looking for. This will help people get out of the ruts they're in and show them the way out of their problems." She was so excited about what she had heard, she immediately called Theodorre saying, "We have to learn more about this Enneagram."

Learning and Teaching the Enneagram

Within a few months of Kathy's return, we had found an Enneagram teacher in Denver and attended her seminars. Soon after that, we created our own notes and began teaching ourselves.

Insights into the nine personality types of the Enneagram

accumulated quickly from talking with people of each type, from observation, and from discussions between ourselves. Almost from the first moment we studied it, the Enneagram promised to lead us into ever-deepening wisdom about humanity, both how human beings are broken and how they are healed. And at each step, it lived up to this promise and more!

More importantly, we began to look at the system as a whole so that we could understand how it is put together and what makes it tick. Soon we realized that the Enneagram is a dynamic, living system. It has never been and will never be a stagnant, rigid set of definitions and characteristics passed on from one generation to another. Instead, it is a vibrant wisdom — evolving, changing, growing.

We also find the Enneagram to be a wisdom that paradoxically grows deeper, yet simpler, the more we use it. That is why we believe it is the most understandable and user-friendly guide to the soul for anyone seeking spiritual development.

We have worked with the Enneagram daily almost since we first learned it. We have dedicated our lives to learning, expanding and teaching these ideas because we have seen them changing lives.

In the course of our research, teaching and personal application of the Enneagram, two things happened that would forever change us. The first was the discovery of the writings of Dr. Maurice Nicoll (1884 – 1953). This great spiritual teacher (who remains unknown to most people today) wrote extensively on working with the three centers of intelligence present in every human being, which we now name by the simple words thinking, feeling and doing. Since the three centers are a part of the Enneagram teaching we had learned, we were attracted to Nicoll's writings.

Working with the three centers and their relationship to the nine types led to the second major breakthrough: being able to see and understand the nine types from the inside out, not just from the outside as the original Enneagram teaching presented them. (We pursue this idea extensively in chapters 1 and 2 under the heading of "center configuration.") At this point, we saw the connection between personality type and discovering soul potential.

A New Life and a New Teaching Emerge

Both of these events changed our personal application of the Enneagram as well as how we taught it. On the personal plane, the insight and compassion created by our new understanding of our very different Enneagram types (Kathy is a Three and Theodorre is a Four), allowed us to relate on ever-deeper levels. It also led us to get married.

From our research and teaching we produced two books, and now our third. We have dedicated our lives to teaching people how to develop the soul using the Enneagram as a tool for growth and change.

We can confidently say we have found the Enneagram to be a firm foundation for spirituality. That is why the

Enneagram is the centerpiece of this book called *Discover Your Soul Potential*. It is a portal to the straightest and surest path to the soul that we have ever found. It is also a mirror to the soul on that journey, serving as a guide to keep the spiritual seeker on the narrow way and not get sidetracked from his or her spiritual goals.

The Enneagram can give you a jump start no matter what spiritual path you follow. Acting like a light shining in a darkened room, it points with clarity to the issues you need to work with and to the strengths you have with which to work on them.

The teachings of Dr. Nicoll and other researchers have now led us beyond the Enneagram. The result is a simple yet complete and detailed path for healing the human soul that begins with knowledge of your Enneagram type. It is based in ancient wisdom sources while also being fully contemporary and adaptable to life in the modern world. Walking this path ourselves, we attempt to support others on the same journey.

CHAPTER 1

THE AWAKENING SOUL

*"In the final analysis, we count for something only
because of the essential we embody, and if we do not
embody that, life is wasted."*

— C. G. Jung

The mystery of how to awaken the potential of the human soul has stirred the imagination and aroused the deepest longing in the hearts of people in every age. When we hear or read about ordinary people who live extraordinary lives of love, compassion, wisdom or service, something within us connects with a greater reality. A secret yearning stirs our own souls.

All too quickly those soul-stirring moments pass. We are drawn back into our daily reality where, at best, we try to find creative new ways of living our lives and managing our relationships with parents, children, partner, co-workers and friends. At worst, we go back to doing what we've always done and wishfully hope that all the tensions and turmoil of our lives will magically disappear.

This is true because most of us are at a loss to know what we could do to effectively improve our lives. *If we knew what to do we would do it.*

From the inside, most of us believe we're doing the best we can. From the outside, other people may see many things we need to change. But on the inside, we usually justify, excuse or explain away each of them. The truth is that we justify our faults because, knowing that we've tried to change them and have failed, we are at a loss regarding how to proceed.

In this state of feeling stuck, we are simultaneously (although we are probably unconscious of doing it) abandoning hope of developing our soul potential. We're allowing ourselves to be caught in the day-to-day cares and anxieties of life and see little if any hope for change. Maybe we have even begun to wonder whether spiritual vitality is a myth.

Six years ago we met Larry. He had just finished reading our book *My Best Self* and since he lived nearby, he telephoned us. At that time we didn't know that his business had failed, he was broke, he was divorced, his relationship with his family of origin was a source of great pain, and he didn't know where to turn. He was connecting with us in the hope of hearing something that would relieve his desperation.

As it happened, we had scheduled the initial meeting of an Enneagram study group the following Saturday, and we invited Larry to join us. That was a turning point in Larry's life. By diligently applying the principles he learned in that group, especially the ideas about the nature of his soul and its three centers of intelligence, Larry gained the soul knowledge and understanding he needed to heal his personal relation-

ships. In a short time, he developed new, fulfilling relationships. Humor, generosity, a welcoming spirit, and spiritual
aliveness soon marked his relationships with everyone.

Larry discovered what all spiritual seekers learn: that
spiritual vitality, the potential of one's own soul, is inextrica-
bly intertwined with the practical realities of our daily lives.
Healthy relationships and spiritual aliveness develop as we
sort out who we really are and how our own souls relate with
their Source. We are spiritual as well as physical beings, and all
our difficulties find their resolution in the realm of spirit when
it is grounded in physical reality.

Then Larry died suddenly. While we were shocked and
saddened at his death, we knew his soul was ready to move on
because he had been doing the inner work necessary to
embrace the fullness of his humanity and develop his soul
potential.

What Is the Soul?

The wisdom that underlies the Enneagram can be of vital
importance in the spiritual lives of all people. For that reason,
we will spend the rest of this chapter exploring that wisdom. It
will support us in making sense out of aspects of life that have
always perplexed us. It will also lay a firm foundation for the
insights that the Enneagram will teach us in the following
chapters of this book.

The wisdom that is foundational to the Enneagram
propels us out of that stuck place where we are caught in the

cares and anxieties of life, and it guides us toward our souls. The Enneagram reveals the relationship between our souls (or true selves) and the experience we have of ourselves daily, which we usually name personality and which, in reality, is a combination of our true personality with our *false personality!*

The Enneagram does this by revealing the daily experience of our inner selves is not random or even chaotic as it may at times seem. Rather, it is ordered, patterned and even automatic to the point of being mechanical.

To understand how human beings work inside, we begin with a simple perception. Human beings have three native intelligences. Called by many different names through the millennia, here we will simply name them the "thinking" intelligence, "feeling" intelligence and "doing" intelligence. Ancient wisdom, which has been verified by modern scientific brain research, affirms this idea. It is virtually a universally accepted precept of the world's philosophies and religions.

To say that human nature is based on thinking, feeling and doing seems so natural it doesn't command our attention. This idea clarifies the issue so much, you think you've always known it. The magnitude of this deceptively simple idea is revealed only when you begin to ponder its implications.

Every day, we use these three faculties to make our way through the world. When faced with a question, project, risk or any new prospect, we naturally ask, "What do I think about it?", "How do I feel about it?", and "What will I do about it?" By focusing these three intelligences *outward,* we create thoughts, feelings, attitudes, skills and reactions that allow us to interact with people and the world in our own way. The name given to the sum total of these qualities is "personality."

However, we also have another experience of these three intelligences. It may happen in a moment of reflection or in a moment of shock; it may come through an artistic experience or through an experience of nature; it may happen as a result of intense focus or delightful relaxation. In truth, it can happen in different ways but when it does, you know it is not an ordinary experience. You know it as an element of life that is deeper than daily experience, something more real.

These are experiences of soul. They emerge from the same three intelligences — thinking, feeling and doing — but operate on a plane of clearer perception, deeper wisdom, more profound presence and *interior* focus. After having an experience like this, many people do not know what it is. Therefore, they don't name it a soul experience or they dismiss it altogether, so that they do not recognize their own soul when they connect with it.

Even more importantly, these random experiences of soul tell us we are not *living* in our souls in a consistent way. Our soul power dissipates because it tends to be unconscious and undeveloped. That is the reason our ordinary experiences of ourselves and our relationships are often disappointing. They cause of much of the pain and frustration we deal with daily. Frequently we don't meet even our own ethical and relational standards because we come from a place within that is less than our true selves, or "less than soul."

Thus, we can say our souls are not strong enough to be present all the time. If they were, then truth, goodness and beauty, which make up the natural environment of our souls, would be far more prevalent in our lives and in our world. We need to develop our soul potential, which we find in the three centers of intelligence.

Thus, the three centers of intelligence can function in two ways. Focused on the outer world, they gain the knowledge we need to live daily life. Focused inwardly, they access our soul potential.

Twentieth Century Messengers of Soul Awareness

George Gurdjieff and Carl Jung, two towering teachers of soul work, were spiritual giants who came from vastly different backgrounds and used almost entirely exclusive sources. Gurdjieff originated the Fourth Way school of spiritual transformation in the west, also called The Work. Jungian psychology largely depends on working with archetypes and analyzes material that rises from the collective unconscious.

Gurdjieff and Jung were contemporaries whose lives began in the last quarter of the nineteenth century and spanned the first half of the twentieth. Although they never met face to face, both men had vitally important messages about the soul for western culture. The style with which each delivered his message was drastically different, yet there were many similarities in the messages themselves.

The Time for Soul Development Is Now

Gurdjieff and Jung both noted that the evolutionary process is no longer as slow as in previous centuries. Therefore, we cannot allow ourselves to sit back and let life unfold by itself. They foretold the unleashing of menacing anti-soul forces in the twentieth century. They believed that with people's increasing pace and exterior focus, western culture could completely lose touch with soul and the interior values of the soul. Both men emphasized that, because of these forces, the time for the work of personal growth is now, not in the future.

They also both believed that we face a *loss of soul awareness* — the loss of connection with the true purpose of the three centers of intelligence, which they believed make us truly human. Thus, they said humanity can actually perish unless we become "real persons" by living in and nurturing our souls.

Although this prediction that our humanness could be extinguished through loss of soul awareness may seem exaggerated, its signs have been escalating in western society just as both men predicted. The growth of violence is probably the most obvious sign, especially because it is accompanied by a lack of appreciation of our common humanity in the eyes of many perpetrators. Veteran psychologists report that every decade shows an increase of severe pathologies in their clients. The ever-increasing challenges our educational systems face not only indicate loss of soul but are seeds of deeper losses in the next generation.

Writing from their vast research in the world's philosophies and religions, both Gurdjieff and Jung believed we are not created with a fully developed soul by virtue of being born on this earth. Rather, we can only become a "real person" by working on our essential self or soul throughout life.

Our soul is created as a spark of the divine yet it is undeveloped. Incarnated, soul interacts with the world and unfolds. Then, as we grow, personality forms as a way for soul to express itself. However, through later childhood and adolescence, personality becomes riveted on the cares and anxieties of the world and slowly slips into the practice of engaging mechanically with the world. This is the birth of false personality, generally equivalent to what Jungian psychology calls "complexes." False personality in effect causes the soul to fall asleep.

What we generally call personality is often an expression of false personality, or the false self, because often our reactions to life are automatic or mechanical. What is mechanical is not free or truly human; it is an escape from essence or soul. From this perspective, transformation becomes the journey from the mechanical reactions of false personality to the truly human responsiveness of the soul.

The Wounding Process

If it is imperative we develop our souls now, it is vital we understand what the soul is, how it is wounded and becomes unconscious, how it is healed, and how its potential is developed. As Jung, Gurdjieff and many others have stated, human beings are created with the soul intact but undeveloped. The intelligences of thinking, feeling and doing are equal and in balance, each ready to be developed for its proper purposes. We are created ready to develop our soul potential.

However, due to the wounding every person necessarily experiences in childhood, we learn to use these intelligences in an *imbalanced* way, creating personality and false personality.

Childhood wounding is inevitable and takes place because of the limitations of life. Every need cannot be met; every tear cannot be wiped away. No one can protect a child from experiencing the hurts that come from interacting with others. Life is a process of wounding and loss on the one hand, and of healing and growth on the other.

A certain level of wounding is even more primal than this. For example, every hello is followed by a good-bye. To an innocent child, good-bye is a loss of connection and could be experienced as a wound. As surely as good experiences begin, they also end; the ending of a pleasurable experience is a loss of a safe, comfortable situation and could be experienced as a wound. As much as caregivers love a child, they will necessarily at times fail in their love; the failure of love is a loss of affirmation by the most important people in a child's tiny world and could be experienced as a wound.

Children are also wounded because *they* love. When

caregivers are under stress or in pain, the child who loves them often wants to help alleviate the pain. Since a child does not have the skills to be nurturing and protective, he or she may find one of the three intelligences wounded in the attempt to take care of what he or she is not capable of caring for.

Children are also wounded because they cannot understand the world in which they live. In complicated situations they often don't have enough information to interpret their experiences correctly or objectively, so they make wrong connections and unhelpful conclusions, which can easily wound one of the three centers.

Caregivers relate to their children from their personal perspective, which by necessity has many flaws that generally are unconscious. It's often out of love, not lack of love, that caregivers influence a child with a wounded part of themselves. This influence can easily damage one of the child's three intelligences not only by harming it on the one hand, but also by inflating it with an unreal sense of its own importance or value on the other.

To this list of the ways people are wounded, add the sad experience of many children — that of deliberate abuse, whether physical, emotional, verbal or spiritual. These experiences deepen the natural wounding process.

Henri Nouwen, spiritual teacher, author, and member of L'Arche community for the mentally retarded, said, "The great tragedy of human love is that it always wounds. Why is this so? Simply because human love is imperfect, always tainted by needs and unfulfilled desires."

The Three Centers of Intelligence

Because of the inevitable wounding children experience, the three centers slowly slip from accessing soul potential to operating for survival. That is why our everyday experience of the three centers is "less than soul."

In daily life, we use the thinking center for gathering and sorting information, planning and analyzing. Its soul capacity includes pondering, objectifying and creating new ideas.

We usually use the feeling center to acknowledge feeling, to acknowledge other people's needs and agendas, and to create and maintain interpersonal relationships. Its soul potential includes artistic creation, experiencing gratitude and creating meaning.

In daily life, we use the doing center for movement, pleasure seeking and accomplishment. Its soul expressions include the experiences of guidance, joy and delight, and inventiveness.

The Three Centers Imbalanced

It's possible that babies first try to understand life through one intelligence and that this center becomes most wounded. It meets the world first and takes the brunt of its limitations and harsh ways. Often, it's trying to make sense out of a tragic, complicated and mystifying world.

When one intelligence is repeatedly wounded early in life, it naturally withdraws to a place of safety, but where it also can't develop. Thus, wounding creates an imbalanced use of the three centers. This imbalance happens on two levels. It is important to note the difference between these two aspects of imbalance and their relationship to each other.

The first level is how we **interpret** the information that **comes into us** through our senses both physical and inner. The second level is how we **process** information, that is, how we make sense of information after we have received and interpreted it. By consistently processing information in a particular way, we create our own personal world view. Because our world view is the basis for our actions, this level reflects **the energy that flows from us.**

Interpreting Information

Though created equal, the centers become unequal as one center moves forward to interpret information received through our physical and inner senses. Eventually, we habitually see and interpret all of life through this center's values.

This happens as a response to our environment. We experience our caregivers and other environmental influences as asking us to deal with life in a certain way to get our needs met and to be loved. We then bring forward the intelligence that will produce the desired response. We call this intelligence the "preferred center."

People who see the world through the thinking center

tend to value information, analysis, logic and discovering patterns. People who see the world through the feeling center generally value emotion, feeling, relationships and interpersonal dynamics. People who see the world through the doing center usually value action, determination, vitality and protecting their own safety.

The preferred center acts as both a lens and as blinders. As a lens, it focuses our attention while distorting the image. As blinders, it treats as unimportant the values of the other two centers. The result is a point of view that sees only a third of what is being experienced. It misinterprets everything because either the wrong center is being used to explain the situation at hand, or the situation requires values that the preferred center does not possess.

For example, we've likely known people who view interpersonal dynamics (feeling center) through logic (thinking center), who respond to a To-Do list (doing center) by selecting what they feel like doing (feeling center) or what interests them (thinking center) and not what needs to be done. Or they charge ahead to accomplish a task (doing center) without considering how it will affect other people (feeling center).

However, when people use the preferred center they are interpreting life *habitually or mechanically*. It would be best if we could interpret life with all three centers as appropriate to the situation — for example, to deal with our checkbook with the thinking center, family relationships with the feeling center, and household chores with the doing center. We create many problems for ourselves by using the wrong center in our attempts to accomplish a task. We do this either because the appropriate center is unavailable or because we are uncomfortable with that center due to childhood wounding.

Processing Information

Interpreting information habitually through one center is the first way we create imbalance within. The second way relates to making sense of the information we have interpreted (or misinterpreted). This happens at the level of processing information, or giving information meaning.

It would be best if we could process information with all three centers. This would yield a complete perspective, and we would have a balanced and appropriate response to life. However, due to the childhood wounding process, the equal use of all three centers becomes impossible. The wounded center fades into the background. It becomes incapable of contributing its values as the person tries to make sense out of the information received. This intelligence we call the "repressed center."

Special information about the repressed center. It is important to note that when a center is repressed, *it hasn't disappeared.* Rather, the strengths of this center are unconscious. As a result, the mechanical and reactive aspects of this intelligence rise up and disrupt our daily lives. Developing the more creative functions of this center becomes a person's lifelong challenge *and* lifelong opportunity for soul expansion. This transformational work creates spiritual vitality.

The repressed center is also the intelligence we use least well, and this fact will be *most apparent in our personal lives.* In our professional lives, we learn to develop those skills we need to get along and get ahead. After leaving the pressures of work, we let our hair down and do what feels most comfortable to us.

Two centers do the work of three. As one intelligence slips into last place in the personality, one of the other two intelligences moves forward to take the lead. The other center follows closely behind in a support role. This leaves us with only two centers to make sense of life. When a person doesn't have free use of all three centers, several things occur.

Because two intelligences are doing the work of three and are therefore overworked, only a few of their values dominate the way information is processed. Soon they are triggering each other in habitual patterns, and the person develops a predictable point of view on many aspects of life.

So, at the level of how people make sense of information, a center takes one of three positions. If it is taking the lead, its values govern the way information is processed. This is called the "dominant center." Closely aligned with the dominant center but in second place is the "support center." The values of this center support the dominant center as information is processed. The center in third place, the repressed center, is being protected and stays relatively dormant.

The Centers Are Not Free

When we look at the analysis described on the previous pages, we realize that the three centers — the three intelligences that are the natural resources of our souls — will never be able to achieve their true purposes in their present states. Operating fully, their energy would point outward, connecting us to the world around us. As a result, each would act independently and therefore appropriately.

Instead, in their average states in our day-to-day lives, their energy points toward each other, creating egocentricity. Thus, their agendas are tangled with each other and none of them can reach its full potential. They are in lockstep. They move together, so that the wrong center becomes involved in the response to the situation. They are like an enmeshed family in which everyone's business is everyone else's business.

The Dominant-Support Center Team

The team of dominant center and support center determines people's values and priorities. These two intelligences become familiar with working together and trigger each other automatically as they make sense out of the impressions received from the world.

There are three team possibilities, each with its strengths and deficits. One team combines the thinking and doing intelligences. People in which this team operates are oriented toward their own ideas and actions; they think and do; they feel free to do what they want or need to do. The thinking and doing centers playing off each other create the "aggressive stance"; from this perspective people feel they can shape the world to be in accord with their image of it. This team leaves out the feeling center, and so people in whom this team operates tend to dismiss the importance of emotions, inter-personal dynamics and other people's agendas.

A second team combines the doing and feeling intelligences. People in which this team operates are oriented toward responding to people and situations; they see a need and try to fill it. These people feel a responsibility to improve the situation. The doing and feeling centers interacting with each other create the "dependent stance"; it allows the immediate situation to determine the person's agenda. This team leaves out the thinking center and so people in whom this team operates tend not to know how to set boundaries, evaluate the situation, evaluate their own performance, or plan their lives.

A third team combines the thinking and feeling intelligences. People in which this team operates are oriented toward their inner life; they appreciate and are at home with intricacy. These people live in their inner world. When the thinking and feeling centers are tangled with each other, it creates the "withdrawing stance"; this inward focus creates comfort with complexity and discomfort with the practical realities of life. This team leaves out the doing center, and people in whom this team operates tend not to be able to think practically, pay little attention to day-to-day responsibilities, and focus their attention on what pleases or interests them.

Nine Types of Personality

Now we can assemble the information on the preceding pages. Because there are three ways of taking in information (or interpreting) and three ways of making sense from information (or processing), there are, from the perspective of the centers of intelligence, nine types of personality. The chart below summarizes these ideas. This is the foundation of the

Why There Are Nine Types

Type	Interpreting Center	Processing Centers
Two	Feeling	Doing and Feeling
Three	Feeling	Thinking and Doing
Four	Feeling	Feeling and Thinking
Five	Thinking	Feeling and Thinking
Six	Thinking	Doing and Feeling
Seven	Thinking	Thinking and Doing
Eight	Doing	Thinking and Doing
Nine	Doing	Feeling and Thinking
One	Doing	Doing and Feeling

Enneagram. The next chapter elaborates on these personality styles, explaining how a different set of motivations, potentials, strengths and deficits arise from the unique way the three centers interrelate within each type.

The Enneagram Interpreted Through the Three Centers

Beginning with this deceptively simple insight, the Enneagram quickly evolves into a system of soul development that supports the spiritual seeker in recreating his or her life. It has that potential because it unites two great sources of human wisdom — ancient spiritual truth and modern insight into personality structure. Separately, these idea systems have already yielded much healing; together, their power to support people in growth is astounding.

Because the Enneagram types are indeed "types," they describe ways of reacting to life that people of each type share with hundreds of millions of other people of the same type. Why are these reactions so predictable? Because they are the automatic and mechanical reactions of *false personality.* They arise from centers triggering each other in predictable ways. Without self-observation, reflection, and a generous dose of inner work, we allow the three centers to function at their lowest and most automatic levels, while we rarely access them for their most exalted, free and responsive qualities — the qualities of soul. But only when we live in our souls do we express our true individuality and discover the unique meaning of our lives.

One Step Further

The Enneagram, in effect, takes the insight of Jung and Gurdjieff one step further. If they said humanity is in peril of losing soul awareness, *the Enneagram describes in specific terms how individual human beings actually lose their soul awareness.* Most importantly, knowledge of this downward movement yields insight about reversing the process.

Therefore, the deeper reasons for discovering your Enneagram type are, first, to ascertain which of the nine ways of losing contact with soul is yours, and second, to shed light on the primary paths that lead back home, back to the depths of your own soul. Your Enneagram type describes your automatic ways of reacting to life, the ways you get hypnotized by the cares and anxieties of the world. Your soul is free, supple, creative and responsive; it stores the lessons you have learned in life along with the lessons yet to be learned. As your automatic reactions dissolve, your soul awakens. You can engage with the world in healthy, life-enhancing ways.

The cause of life's dilemmas is that we misuse the resources of our own human natures! By taking responsibility for the natural resources of our own beings — the intelligences of thinking, feeling and doing — we find that the power to change lies in our own power to choose. If false personality is created by an imbalance of three moveable centers, you can realign them and balance them to discover the wonder of your soul, especially by developing the intelligence you least favor.

Healing From the Inside Out

This "balancing through inclusion" is a movement of healing. When people face their type squarely, they see how its excesses, incorrect perceptions and wrong judgments limit them. Often, their first response is to rub off the rough edges. But if you have a strong thinking center, for example, why would you want to bring down its functioning? Instead, build up what is weakest. To do otherwise is self-defeating because it's based on a judgment and a fundamental antagonism with oneself. It's being less of who you really are.

By discovering that an imbalanced use of centers (and especially repressing one center) creates your false personality, the solution to your problem becomes exploring the strengths of the underdeveloped intelligence. In doing so, you expand your horizons, gain new talents and strengths, and come to live from a place of security and strength. To the degree that all three centers are developed and ready to contribute their best to life, the problems that your Enneagram type creates slowly dissolve. Balancing through inclusion means you become less of who you are not and more of who you really are!

Working with the three centers is the most practical way to grow spiritually, psychologically and relationally in everyday life. It also has the advantage of being an inclusive, *nonviolent* approach to healing both individuals and society. The self-judgment and dislike that are the foundation of rubbing off our rough edges are, in truth, violence toward ourselves.

That inner violence creates outer violence in our relationships and, by extension, in our families, our communities and
in society itself. Learning to access the higher expressions of
all three centers, by its very nature, eliminates the excesses of
the style of any Enneagram type. It contributes to the expression of positive energy for the healing of our communities and
of society.

Discovering Your Soul

The Enneagram is best understood and applied in the
context of soul work — growing your soul, learning to live a
soul-filled life, correctly using the three centers of intelligence, and finding and following the unique meaning of your
soul.

Although every human soul is composed of the same
three intelligences, tradition gives each of the nine types a
unique face of God or divine image to express. To the degree
that the three centers operate freely, we express our divine
image and therefore experience the divine purpose for our
lives. We have dealt extensively with these divine images in
our previous books, and we will not repeat that information
here. However, the name of the divine image for each type is
included in the section that summarizes information about
that type as well as in the glossary of this book.

If you want to consult our descriptions of these divine
images, see chapter 8 (pages 151 – 167)of *What's My Type?*
Use the Enneagram System of Nine Personality Types to Discover

Your Best Self (Harper San Francisco, 1992) and chapter 7 (pages 205 – 232) of *My Best Self: Using the Enneagram to Free the Soul* (Harper San Francisco, 1993). Allow the descriptions of your divine image to inspire you to pursue the daily hard work of personal transformation.

By seeing and owning your type — your particular way of having become lost and alienated from the truth of who you are — you can find your way back home: back to the place where you began your journey, back to the Source. As T. S. Eliot's poem "Four Quartets" reflects:

> *We shall not cease from exploration*
> *And the end of all our exploring*
> *Will be to arrive where we started*
> *And know the place for the first time.*

CHAPTER 2

THE SOUL POTENTIAL
OF THE NINE ENNEAGRAM TYPES

"After all, what is your personal identity? It is what
you really are, your real self. None of us is what we
think we are, or what other people think we are . . . .
Many of us think, no doubt, that we are what we
would like to be. And it is fortunate for most of us that
we are mistaken."

— Thomas Merton

Native Americans tell the tale of a warrior who climbed to the top of a mountain where he found an eagle's egg. Foolishly, he carried the egg down the mountain. Then, not knowing what else to do with the egg, he placed it among eggs being hatched by a chicken.

In time, the chicks and the eaglet broke through their shells. The eaglet grew up with the chickens, learning to cluck like all the others. Soon he was squawking, scratching and clawing at the earth, pecking for worms and searching for enough food to appease his hunger for another day. In due time, he learned to flap his wings just enough to perch on the low branches of a nearby tree with all the other chickens.

Time passed until one day, when the eagle had grown to full size, he happened to look up and see a magnificent sight. In the clear, deep blue sky, a majestic bird effortlessly glided on the strong currents of wind. The eagle felt his heart leap as he watched the bird with awe and he was profoundly impressed. Slowly turning to the oldest chicken, he asked, "Who is that?"

"That?" said the chicken looking first toward the sky and then at the eagle. "That's the Golden Eagle, the king of the birds. But don't waste your time thinking about him. You and I are chickens and we need to worry about finding enough food to get by each day."

The End of the Story

How does the story of the eagle end? The answer may surprise you: for each person who hears it, the story ends differently! Because stories like this one are intended to teach us something important about life, we each complete the story in the way we will complete our own lives.

We have all likely had experiences like that of the eagle looking at the sky. Maybe we have met someone who inspired us, or we have seen a happy person, couple or family and were profoundly impressed. A beautiful piece of music or a magical painting or photograph may touch us whenever we experience it. Maybe our heart leaps as we watch a child at play. In these experiences, a deeper, more real part of us longs to be free, to live our essential truth. However, that's when the old chicken within usually reminds us not to waste our time thinking about such things because we have to scratch out a living.

It's at precisely this point the Enneagram can be most helpful. The Enneagram can unleash our power to soar like an eagle instead of live like a chicken. That's because it reveals the "chicken habits" (false personality) that cover up our "eagle nature" (soul).

We do many things out of habits formed so long ago that we can't remember or imagine being different. Called our false personality, these habits prevent us from seeing both solutions to our everyday problems on the practical side and the true nature of our souls on the transcendent side.

Even a glorious golden eagle will live, eat, sleep and die like a chicken if he believes he's a chicken and takes on a chicken's habits. The Enneagram describes nine possible ways we can act like chickens instead of the eagles we were meant to be. It guides us to our souls.

The Role of the Enneagram

The Enneagram peers beneath the inclinations and characteristics we express daily to decipher what creates our responses to life. The Enneagram reflects the structure of the everyday intelligence with which we perceive and handle reality, both inside and out. By definition, a person can have only one structure to his or her intelligence.

It's like body type: If you are five-feet- five-inches tall with a square, sturdy bone structure, no amount of stretching exercises or dieting will make you six-foot-two-inches tall with a slender body. However, exercise and diet will tone and increase your natural physical attributes.

Because the Enneagram is about the structure of everyday intelligence, a person's Enneagram type does not change. Rather, it is open to different expressions that access either more creative or destructive aspects of the type. The Enneagram discloses the core motivation (which is generally unconscious) that drives the personality and perpetuates its habitual responses to life.

While the Enneagram describes nine motivations, it acknowledges many different kinds of people. These differences combine the many factors that come into play as people develop. They include variables such as genetics, upbringing, relative depth of childhood wounding, education both formal and informal, birth order, personal choices, etc. Consequently, every person is unique.

Patterned Thought, Feeling and Behavior

But don't allow the idea that each person is unique convince you that any of us is "free." The Enneagram shows that, without conscious choice to be different, the centers act habitually and trigger each other in fixed ways. By describing the results of these patterned interactions among the centers, the Enneagram shows that freedom is an illusion until we "work" on ourselves.

However, when you understand how type is created by the

tangled interaction of the three centers, you immediately see how to allow the compulsive aspects of type to dissolve. By recognizing the problem, you can alleviate the negative personal qualities and unhelpful responses that the Enneagram describes.

Discovering Your Type

Someone commented after an Enneagram seminar years ago, "This system tells you more about yourself than you ever wanted to know." It is a clear mirror that reflects exactly how you are thinking, feeling and behaving, mostly to your own detriment. That's why, upon learning the Enneagram, many people say it can be a difficult truth to swallow. In this book, we have attempted to counterbalance the negative aspects of type by pointing out positive characteristics in each type, and by showing a way out of the difficulties that each type experiences.

As we describe the nine types of the Enneagram, you may easily recognize the types of the other people in your life before you see yourself. To determine your own type, keep these points in mind.

1. Take each type as a whole. Don't decide you are a particular type because of a few qualities you recognize in yourself. For example, you'll see that Fours have an artistic temperament. However, this statement doesn't mean that all Fours are artists or that all artists are Fours.

2. Notice which types attract or repel you. Often we are attracted to our own type because we enjoy being the way we are, or we are repelled by our own type because we're given to a consistently self-critical attitude.

3. If you're the kind of person who has worked at personal growth, think of yourself in your younger years, for compulsions are more obvious earlier in life.

4. Remember, this is not a multiple choice quiz! You don't get to pick the type that is most appealing to you or that you think is most acceptable to others.

5. A checklist of 12 characteristic attitudes accompany each type description. Use it to help you pinpoint your type.

6. As you discover which type is yours, keep in mind that all the types are equally strong and weak, wonderful and terrible, admirable and reprehensible. *It's not which type you are but what you do with it that counts.*

7. As you learn about your type, you may recognize in yourself a characteristic you dislike, find embarrassing or are ashamed of. Remember that many strengths and gifts accompany that weakness.

8. If you identify with personal qualities that you don't like in your type, remember that discovering your type is only the first step in your journey. Realize that growth is not only possible but also easily accessible in everyday life.

9. Tips on developing positive qualities and minimizing weaknesses are built into each type description.

The Enneagram of Personality

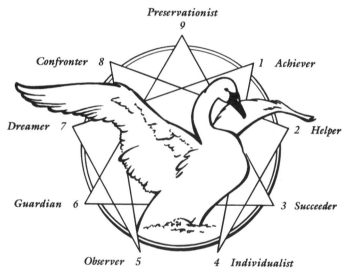

Preservationist
9

Confronter 8

1 Achiever

Dreamer 7

2 Helper

Guardian 6

3 Succeeder

Observer 5

4 Individualist

ONE: THE ACHIEVER

Quick Overview

Thumbnail sketch. Ones are highly focused and intense people who measure everything — especially themselves and their own performance — by perfectionistic standards. Often presenting the smiling, sociable side of their personalities to the world, they experience great interior pressure to work hard and be fair, moderate, just, kind and amiable as well. They tend to think in black/white, either/or terms and can become rigid.

Ones keep a tight rein on their emotions, especially anger, to attain the perfectly acceptable response. An insistent mental voice criticizes them if they do not live up to all their standards; often it causes them to criticize others. Ones feel caught in imperfection so strive to avoid it; they want to feel perfect.

Positive descriptors. Dedicated, ethical, hard working, reliable, practical, conscientious, disciplined, responsible, honest, fair, idealistic, creative.

Negative descriptors. Self-righteous, moralistic, judgmental, critical, resentful, perfectionistic, puritanical, rigid, angry, intense, dogmatic, myopic.

Checklist

If you are a One, it's likely that you:

☐ Obey (or fight with) an inner voice that points out your

faults and mistakes and tells you how you could have done things better.

☐ Measure everything — especially yourself and your own performance — by exacting standards because there is a right and wrong way to do everything.

☐ Work long and hard, and expect others to do the same, but feel guilty if you say so because you also feel you must be kind, amiable and fair toward others.

☐ Have to finish all your work before you can play, but somehow all the work never seems to get done.

☐ Tend to make To-Do lists — either verbal or written— for yourself and others.

☐ Have to meet all needs of the people around you before you can meet your own and therefore usually put yourself last on your own list.

☐ Often feel resentment, which you try to mask so that others don't see or feel it.

☐ Reflect on issues until you can state your conclusion with the conviction that you are right.

☐ Believe that, because you've thought it through so clearly, your way is usually the right and best way to do something.

☐ Encourage others to be as responsible as you feel you are.

☐ Are a high energy person who desires to get a lot done.

☐ Are a private person who is guarded in conversation lest you reveal more about yourself than you want others to know.

What's Going On Inside

Center configuration. Ones see the world through the doing center and therefore *interpret* life through the values of determination, action and protecting themselves. They *process* information with the feeling and doing intelligences, which orients their interest toward how well they respond to a particular situation. Because their thinking center is repressed, they are unable to evaluate their performance so they try their best in every situation hoping to achieve excellence. They mechanically respond to life by being dedicated and working hard to excel in every project they undertake.

Doing Is Preferred

Focus on their response to life
See themselves as good only
when exerting effort

Interior pressure to work hard
Need to live up to standards
Need to improve the world

Thinking Is Repressed

Overcritical inner voice
Perfectionists
Overanalyze
Can't get the big picture
Opinionated

Feeling Supports Doing

Emotionally attached to what they
do and how they do it
Personal likes and dislikes
dominate their lives

Preferred center and dominant center. Because the doing center is preferred in Ones, they see life in terms of responsibilities and work. Simultaneously using the doing center to make sense out of life, they focus their energy directly in front of them. Ones pressure themselves to perform faultlessly in every situation. They have To-Do lists that never end. They insist on perfection, myopically focus on details, and feel a need to improve the world. Ones' intense tenacity for their projects often requires they sacrifice their personal needs for rest and relaxation.

They release the inner pressure created by such intensity only by taking time away from their responsibilities. But as a One said to us, "It's not relaxing for me to goof off because the tension builds and I just feel guilty about all the things I should be doing at home or at the office." Their right-and-wrong, black-and-white approach to life, which can cause others to view them as rigid, superior or stubborn, is tempered by their high personal standards of honesty, integrity, justice and moral character.

Support center. While the feeling center supports the doing center, this does not mean that Ones are emotional people. Although they can be sociable, relational and accommodating to others' needs, Ones have an emotional attachment to their actions. They feel deeply about what they do and how well they do it, which does not leave much feeling energy left for relationships. When things don't turn out the way Ones think they should, they can easily slip into a downward spiral of negative feelings that shift quickly from self-blame to self-justification to blaming others, resulting in resentment, anger and guilt.

Repressed center. Ones repress the thinking center, which usually comes as a surprise to them because they experience themselves as thinking all the time. But that's precisely the point: Ones think nonproductively by looking at situations from all sides several times and overanalyzing them. They find it difficult to separate one issue from another and deal with one thing at a time.

Ones often experience their underdeveloped thinking center as a relentless voice in their minds that criticizes, finds fault, and overemphasizes even minor mistakes. This "inner critic" is thinking at its worst; it dismisses all truly rational and logical arguments by upholding limitless standards of excellence. As a way of compensating for the uncomfortable feeling their spinning minds create, Ones may value and collect credentials (outer validation of thinking), including graduate degrees.

First Steps in Soul Development

Reclaiming full personhood in type One begins by separating the doing and feeling centers so each can achieve its true purpose. In compulsion, the feeling center's qualities are primarily used to support the doing center's agenda — accomplishment, achievement, drive and purposefulness.

As Ones develop the deeper values of the feeling center,

they allow themselves the luxury of personal and intimate relationships, artistic creation, and relationship with the transcendent values of the universe and the divine. This frees them to experience the greater fulfillment and meaning in life that comes with soul development. Then the highly developed gifts of their doing center will no longer be held in bondage to unconscious negative emotional states. They also experience the doing center's wisdom of knowing when *not* to do something. Creative leisure results.

Finally, as Ones learn to trust their impressions and thinking process, they feel less need to overanalyze every situation. They create space in their very active lives, their inner view broadens, and they give time and energy to all the important aspects of their lives, not just to work.

Expression of balance. As Ones move toward the goal of transformation, they become patient.

The Formula for the Passion of Anger

The preferred doing center causes Ones to prize hard work and accomplishment. Their feeling center supports the doing center, which means they have deep feelings about what they do. They also compulsively control their emotions so they can make the perfect response to any situation. Their repressed thinking center prevents them from evaluating how well they do, from setting boundaries around work, or from setting limits on what they can expect from themselves and others.

The only result of this combination of energies could be anger, a nagging resentment that leads to being overly critical and judgmental — attitudes they compulsively keep to a slow burn just under the surface of their daily lives.

Core Strengths

▶ Ones lead through dedication to excellence and clarity of focus.

▶ They are able to see the potential in people and situations and work diligently to bring these aptitudes into reality.

▶ Their high ideals create appreciation of fairness and justice.

▶ Their discipline, honesty and high moral character motivate others to strive for a higher level of commitment and responsibility.

▶ Ones inspire cooperation through personal loyalty and a deep appreciation for the value of the individual.

▶ Ones work hard and pursue a quiet but persistent course of action.

Potential Obstacles

▶ When Ones are preoccupied with what is wrong, they do not recognize or appreciate all that is right.

▶ They can become too attached to a single perception of how something should be done and then rigidly close down to new possibilities or ideas.

▶ They can be overly critical, resentful and demanding.

► When they are enmeshed in details, they lose the overall picture and ignore important tasks.

► They easily develop a self-righteous morality that becomes an intrusive, unbending yardstick by which others are judged.

► For Ones, resentment, intolerance and perfectionism can become constant, harmful emotional attitudes.

Ways to Develop Relationships and Spiritual Vitality

► Set aside time regularly for the sole purpose of expanding and clarifying your overall vision and direction.

► Open to new ideas and possibilities.

► Examine the possibility that you set unreachable standards of perfection and therefore have become a source of irritation and resentment for both you and others.

► Take time to learn about different philosophies that could challenge and expand your current attitudes and perceptions.

► Lighten up, relax and develop your sense of humor.

► Take the initiative to plan something fun with someone you care about.

► Work at becoming an objective thinker who can trust and value the natural process of growth and development.

► Find ways to appreciate people, lifestyles and values different from yours.

Wound

Ones' thinking center is most damaged; consequently, betrayal is the wound of the One. Early on, Ones learned the information they received could not be trusted. As children, often the untrustworthy information was as simple as being expected to act in a proper, adult fashion. They came to believe their safety and happiness depended on not being in the way, not being a burden to anyone. Verbally or nonverbally, Ones were told it was important to be "nice" to others, to act "grown up," to do a "good job" to help lighten the load of others. This way of living became their ticket to receiving approval and love.

Ones often grow up too quickly — often taking parental responsibility for their siblings or even for their own parents. Having learned to be responsible, Ones perpetuate the betrayal wound in adulthood by intensely focusing on their own efforts and never "wasting" time, especially on themselves. They count only on themselves to get a job done right. They are inevitably angry about their situation but because they learned as children that anger is unacceptable, they control their feelings and follow the rules.

Ones also perpetuate their wound of betrayal by believing other people will always let them down, so it's best to go it alone. Depending only on themselves, they spend needless hours overworking, overinvestigating, overrationalizing and overanalyzing. This habit of cyclical thinking helps explain why Ones usually prefer to have limited options, rules, and a rigid standard of right and wrong to guide them.

Healing the wound involves activities that awaken the thinking center. Reading books and articles that ignite new thoughts and ideas regarding the true meaning of life is a good exercise. Discussing these ideas with others develops thinking and keeps the ideas alive. Breathing meditations can focus and quiet their minds. Noticing when irritability or pickiness begin to rise and consciously choosing to refocus on something positive interrupts habitual patterns. It awakens the soul.

Repressed Virtue

The virtue that Ones find most difficult to develop is faith, which, along with hope and love, is key to the process of healing the soul and finding wholeness. Because of childhood wounding, the natural capacity to trust others became unconscious. With their desire to trust others unfulfilled, they learned to resent a world they believe forces them to make up for its untrustworthiness by being overly responsible.

Faith, like all great virtues, takes root in childhood. To have faith does not primarily mean believing in ideas or doctrines. Rather, it means believing *in someone*. Early on in life, Ones decided they could not depend on anyone but themselves.

The opposite of faith is not disbelief but distrust and the kind of fear that causes someone to hold fast to many small beliefs. To compensate for the repression of faith, Ones adopt attitudes like rules, "shoulds," perfectionistic standards, rigid rights and wrongs, and an intensely serious approach to life.

The rebirth of faith in Ones begins in trusting their own impressions of life, then learning to trust others, forgiving them when they fail in trustworthiness. It continues in accepting their own limitations and forgiving themselves. They also can learn to trust the situation and not be so intense in manipulating it to improve it. These inner movements free them to flow with divine energy until their souls trustingly reconnect with the Source of all wisdom.

Forgotten Child

In Ones, the bright, curious, questioning child receded into the background while taking responsibility and exerting effort became more and more important to their egos. Any curious child can, at times, be a pest by stretching limits and getting into trouble. Yet, when this child can trust that he or she is loved in spite of, or perhaps because of, this impishness, the child will continue to search, discover and be filled with the wonder of life.

As children, Ones did not allow themselves to make trouble, be an intrusion, or act impishly. They learned that never being a pest was the way to make other people happy. By trusting themselves to work hard and figure life out as they went along, they felt safe.

Reclaiming and integrating this forgotten aspect of themselves takes time spent in relaxation. Questioning their rigid standards and surrendering the demands they place on themselves lead to a new sense of purpose, meaning and freedom.

Orientation to Time

Ones are tyrannized by the demands of the immediate. Staying focused on the situation before them compensates for the lost virtue of faith or trust, for people don't need to have faith to deal with the here and now.

Ones feel they will finally have time for themselves when the present situation stops demanding all their time. But time for themselves will only arrive when they consciously choose to create it. Then new dreams can be born. Courage will increase as they let go of the familiar and trust in the unknown. Thus they plant themselves in the land of soul.

Challenge

The most important quest for Ones is to become the assertive, wise guide of their own destiny. Their preferred doing center and support feeling center work together to make them perfectionists. However, because they repress the thinking center, Ones allow other people to set their agenda, which means they don't reap the harvest of their own hard work; it's all done to please others or meet their needs. This is the root of the anger they constantly deal with.

Ones are aware of the limitations of their approach to life. They don't trust their thinking until they touch a higher expression of self through spiritual practice. Then, by placing confidence in the will of the higher self rather than the will of their compulsive personality, they are able to set an agenda that allows time to regain the creative freedom that is their birthright.

With the values of the soul guiding them, they are able to regulate their world and cease being controlled by circumstance. They allow the voice of intuition to rise and refine their sense of discrimination and discernment. By balancing their lives, wisdom rises and the critical inner voice fades into silence.

Summary of Type One

Avoidance. Imperfection.

Passion. Anger.

Preferred center. Doing center.

Dominant center. Doing center.

Support center. Feeling center.

Repressed center. Thinking center.

Stance. Dependent.

Orientation to time. Immediate.

Wound. Betrayal.

Repressed virtue. Faith.

Forgotten child. Bright, curious, questioning child.

Divine image. Wisdom.

Questions for Reflection for Ones

1. In what specific ways does holding on to resentments and anger undermine my relationship with myself and others?

2. When I become angry because others are not doing their fair share, how might I creatively and relationally resolve the issue?

3. How would my life and relationships be more fulfilling if I placed limits on the time I spent working?

4. What are the qualities and gifts in others that I most admire, and what prevents me from developing my own version of these attributes?

5. What are the anxieties or fears that cause me to automatically resist change?

6. How might listening to a new idea or a different standard than my own and asking open-minded questions broaden my understanding and acceptance of life and people?

7. What values would I most like to be known for, and what concrete steps can I take now to develop them?

Two: The Helper

Quick Overview

Thumbnail sketch. Of all the Enneagram types, Twos are the most sensitive to human feeling and need. Focusing their energy outward, they respond to the needs of others. Twos need the appreciation and approval of others to feel good about themselves. As perceptive and responsive as they are to others, they are relatively blind to their own needs and weaknesses. The affirming, supportive nature of Twos becomes a mirror through which others are able to see and accept their own strengths and shortcomings.

Their emphasis on the interpersonal dimension can not only lead to dependent relationships, but it can also distract Twos from completing projects or meeting necessary deadlines. They are caught in their own unmet personal needs and strive to avoid them. Not centered in themselves, they need to feel needed by others.

Positive descriptors. Supporting, nurturing, generous, thoughtful, friendly, affirming, empathic, caring, vivacious, perceptive, responsive, diplomatic, good communicators.

Negative descriptors. Opportunistic, manipulative, parochial, patronizing, superior, ingratiating, long-suffering, intruding, flattering, possessive, placating, advice givers.

Checklist

If you are a Two, it's likely that you:

- [ ] Believe the way of service is the most valid way to live.
- [ ] Are able to respond to most any human need presented to you.
- [ ] Believe most people aren't grateful enough for all that you do for them.
- [ ] Naturally focus on other people and their interests in conversations rather than talk about yourself.
- [ ] Comment so as not to hurt other people or put them on edge.
- [ ] Use words to maintain distance when another person becomes too pushy.
- [ ] Are aware of other people's sensitive areas and use that ability either to help them or, if they do something offensive or hurtful, comment to temper their behavior.
- [ ] Find that other people depend on you and you can feel overburdened in these relationships.
- [ ] Believe the world would benefit if others chose the way of service as you do.
- [ ] Are known for your personal approach to problems but not necessarily for your objectivity.
- [ ] Prefer group process and stand by decisions that emerge from it.
- [ ] Take a long time to make decisions so others won't be hurt or disappointed by a rash decision.

What's Going On Inside

Center configuration. Twos see the world through the feeling center, which means they *interpret* life through emotional and relational values. They *process* information with the feeling and doing intelligences, which makes them responsive to the situation. Thus, they are mechanically warm and relational as they respond to life. Because their thinking center is repressed, they are prevented from questioning whether their immediate response to every person and situation is even appropriate.

Preferred center and dominant center. Feeling is the

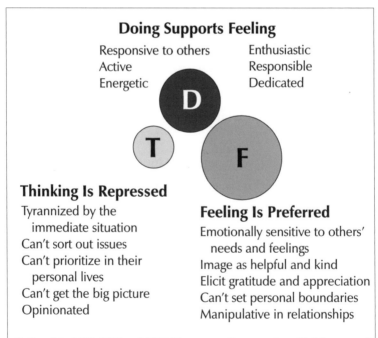

Doing Supports Feeling

Responsive to others   Enthusiastic
Active   Responsible
Energetic   Dedicated

Thinking Is Repressed
Tyrannized by the
  immediate situation
Can't sort out issues
Can't prioritize in their
  personal lives
Can't get the big picture
Opinionated

Feeling Is Preferred
Emotionally sensitive to others'
  needs and feelings
Image as helpful and kind
Elicit gratitude and appreciation
Can't set personal boundaries
Manipulative in relationships

preferred/dominant center in Twos. Their magnetic smile and positive disposition attracts people to them. With their extraordinary emotional sensitivity guiding them, Twos can ascertain instantaneously how best to support and respond to others. Their image of being generous, helpful and kind is of paramount importance to them because they are unaware they have any value aside from that image. Twos' sense of personal identity derives from the respect and appreciation they receive from others. Because Twos are natural caregivers, they see themselves as independent. They fail to recognize that giving to others is fueled by an unconscious need to be needed, which makes them, in fact, dependent on others.

Support center. The support doing center in Twos drives their emotional energy outward. Doing center energy can easily be recognized in their active schedules, spontaneity and enthusiasm for life. Responding to whatever anyone wants or needs is so automatic for Twos that they periodically push themselves to the point of exhaustion. Their actions are motivated by their emotions. Because doing supports feeling in this type, Twos' intense emotional need to be needed by others dictates that little, if any, energy is left to take care of themselves, nor is any time left just to rest.

Repressed center. The evidence of a repressed thinking center in Twos is their dismissal of the values of planning, setting and sticking to a schedule, and having goals for their lives. Their inability to sort out issues or set practical boundaries around the amount of time they give to others directly results from overusing the feeling and doing centers and underusing the thinking intelligence. As a Two said to us, "I understand what boundaries are; I just can't understand why anyone would want to set them." Since their interest is in people, logic and objectivity can seem cold and heartless. Also, they tend to reiterate long-held opinions and attitudes because it's easier than thinking things through for themselves.

First Steps in Soul Development

Reclaiming the true nature for type Two begins in separating the team of the feeling center (sensitivity to human needs) from the support doing center (action orientation). External feeling must diminish so that internal feeling can be developed for its true purposes of mutual (not a one-sided "you need me") relationship, maturing spiritual intuition, and connecting with the larger realities of the universe and the divine.

Their doing center needs to be freed to experience its full range of qualities; Twos need to play, rest and create so that they can experience and express their true selves. They also need to assert themselves appropriately, regulating their energy and stamina so they can also complete their own projects and serve their own life goals.

The third step requires they explore and strengthen their thinking center. This means naming and prioritizing goals, making a plan for the day and keeping it, setting and sticking to boundaries, and questioning their attitudes about life and opinions about others. In understanding and accepting the rationale behind the importance of creative leisure, they will have time to explore new possibilities and ponder the values that lie hidden in their deeper selves.

Expression of balance. As Twos move along on the path of transformation, they become humble.

The Formula for the Passion of Pride

Because the feeling center is out front in Twos, they are always aware of human feeling and need. The doing center supports feeling by acting on this awareness, which makes them look good in the world. Lagging far behind is the repressed thinking center, the intelligence that sees clearly and objectively. Without it working properly, Twos are blind to their own feelings, needs, faults and even their true virtues.

The combination of these attitudes can only result in pride. By taking care of others but not allowing others to take care of them and by giving in order to receive, their egos become identified with their saintly role. They believe they've earned and deserve the gratitude they so abundantly receive.

Core Strengths

▶ Twos lead through appreciation of and communication with people.

▶ They are able to identify what motivates people and support them in developing their highest potential.

► Possessing a contagious energy and enthusiasm, they inspire confidence in and dedication for achieving common organizational or community goals.

► Their consistent focus on the value of people and the ideal of service creates an atmosphere of well-being for everyone.

► Their responsive and warm nature is the basis for their well-developed communication abilities and teaching skills.

► Possessing stellar interpersonal skills and a genuine interest in others, they establish multiple relationships with socially prominent and powerful people who can benefit a community or an entire organization.

Potential Obstacles

► Twos may become distracted by relational concerns and move on to a new task without completing projects already underway.

► They can be so focused on the interpersonal dimension, they either fail to get the big picture or lose sight of the goals and objectives needed to move towards completing the broader vision.

► When they feel unappreciated or taken for granted, they can take on the persona of the martyr and lose their energy and enthusiasm.

► Their need to connect with people can create a smothering and/or manipulative atmosphere that stifles others' freedom to communicate in a direct manner, especially if what needs to be said is a criticism.

► Their tendency to make decisions based on feeling rather than logic can not only produce negative results but can also become a source of family, community or organizational conflict.

► Being overly caring and supportive can prevent others from taking responsibility for themselves and block the spirit of creative initiative from developing in an individual, family, community or organization.

Ways to Develop Relationships and Spiritual Vitality

► Practice "impulse control" by waiting a few hours or even days before rushing to the assistance of someone you feel may need your help.

► Notice when your needs for interaction and appreciation begin to irritate or alienate other people; make a conscious choice to respect their agendas.

► Make a plan for your day and follow it.

► Get an answering machine, screen your phone calls, and allot only a certain amount of time at the end of the day to make your return calls.

► Practice communicating your needs directly; your tendency to be indirect can cause others to feel manipulated and prevent you from getting your real needs met.

► Make a list of your unfinished projects, prioritize them,

and set a time line to complete each one.

➤ Learn and practice meditation and journaling.

➤ As you withdraw from your unconscious caregiving role, others may easily feel unhappy because they have counted on you taking care of them. To alleviate pressure and maintain your boundaries, take an assertiveness training course.

Wound

The core wound in Twos is betrayal. The information they received as children was distorted and could not be trusted; this information could have been as simple as seeing that others could have needs but they could not. Twos learned they got approval for helping, giving, and being sweet, funny and charming but not for being their real selves. Their wound of betrayal deepened as they were made to feel guilty and selfish if they expressed any needs or did things to please themselves.

The message was they couldn't trust themselves; their needs and feelings didn't matter. What they thought was not only unimportant but inaccurate. Since they couldn't trust themselves, their only recourse was to trust others. Others would tell them what was valuable.

Thus, focusing on others intently and being intuitively sensitive to what they needed became their way of survival in childhood. They perpetuate the wound in adulthood by betraying themselves as they live the lie that they can't trust themselves. Because of the original wound of betrayal, their lives are shaped by the false belief they deserve to be loved only for what they give, not for who they are.

Healing this wound begins when Twos develop and strengthen their thinking center. Left on the playground of childhood, this intelligence needs the attention of reading serious nonfiction like psychology or spirituality and applying it to their own lives, not to others'. Time spent pursuing their personal interests and delineating their own life goals and accomplishing them draws their external focus inward. They heal their wound by establishing the identity of their soul or true self.

Repressed Virtue

Of the three key virtues of faith, hope and love, faith or trust is most difficult for Twos. The possibility of having faith in something greater than yourself is damaged if your ability to trust yourself at even the most basic level is obstructed. Twos, who generally aren't encouraged to trust even their most fundamental instincts, have little ground upon which to grow the virtue of faith.

For compulsive Twos, trusting themselves is totally conditional: it depends on making themselves needed through giving to others. They are shackled to the standard of pleasing others in order to feel self-respect. But this kind of self-esteem quickly drains away as the next need arises. If they don't meet every need, they feel guilty and selfish.

Until Twos create time to focus on deeply breathing life

into themselves and allowing the mystery of spirit to flow through them, they will remain confined in a lack of imagination that is fueled by anticipating others' needs. They are distracting themselves from their inner quandary by constant activity. When they quiet themselves enough to enter the mystery of silence, they will discover that the greatest relationship of all is that of the soul with its Source.

Forgotten Child

The bright, curious, questioning child was left behind and forgotten as Twos learned that their own thoughts, feelings, needs and desires weren't dependable. The inner guidance that would have developed through the questioning part of themselves receded as emotional sensitivity and responsibility came forward to help them feel safe and loved in the world.

Twos awaken and reclaim the treasures of this eager and inquisitive part of themselves each time they resist the urge to seek validation externally and, instead, search for it within. Developing reciprocal relationships, identifying needs and vulnerabilities, learning to receive freely, and recognizing their personal worth is based on *who they are* and not on *what they do* — all of these are ways Twos can allow a little child to lead them to the land of soul.

Orientation to Time

Twos allow the needs or desires of the person directly in front of them to dictate their priorities. Thus, Twos are tyrannized by the immediate. Allowing themselves to remain trapped in the "now" protects Twos from facing the difficulties resulting from their wound of betrayal. You don't need faith or trust to deal with the immediate. There's no need to ponder life and question yourself when you've learned to define your identity through consistent response to others' needs. As Twos' underlying issues are resolved, they can live from their souls in the authentic present moment.

Challenge

The most important quest for Twos is the journey inward. Believing they are compelled to *do* something about what they feel, they remain active and take little time for personal reflection. If they take time by themselves, they often fill it with thoughts about others and ideas about how they can be helpful. Because they are also proud of being active and caring, they often don't see the darker side of their own motivation, nor do they admit that the results of their actions in their own lives and in the lives of others are not always positive and constructive.

Twos recover their souls by dealing with the conflict and suffering that comes in facing their own unconscious darker side. The unconscious mind is like a gold mine: a ton of ore yields an ounce of pure gold; the gold not only pays for itself but also makes the miner rich.

When Twos bring awareness to their emotions, thoughts and actions, they first have to walk through a valley of fear that says without their generous caring for others, they are unlovable. This stage is comparable to the ore being refined and the gold being separated from common minerals. Only after facing down their fear do they find the nugget of gold — peace with themselves and the joy that comes when they allow themselves to be loved by others.

Summary of Type Two

Avoidance. Personal needs and feelings.

Passion. Pride.

Preferred center. Feeling.

Dominant center. Feeling.

Support center. Doing.

Repressed center. Thinking.

Stance. Dependent.

Orientation to time. Immediate.

Wound. Betrayal.

Repressed virtue. Faith.

Forgotten child. Bright, curious, questioning child.

Divine image. Understanding.

Questions for Reflection for Twos

1. What are the specific projects in my life that are only partially completed, and what of lasting value prevents me from completing them?

2. What prevents me from journaling about my own needs and feelings, and what would I need to change?

3. How am I manipulating others by communicating indirectly, and what do I gain from speaking this way?

4. What are the issues that make me critical of others, why am I attached to them, and how would letting go of them create freedom for me and others?

5. What dreams or goals did I have for my life that I never fulfilled, and what can I do today to make them come true?

6. If someone asked me to make a list of my needs, desires and wants that would not include the needs of others, what would it contain?

7. What are ten gifts that a bright, curious, questioning child might develop in a healthy way and would contribute to society?

THREE: THE SUCCEEDER

Quick Overview

Thumbnail sketch. What you see when meeting a Three is an energetic, upbeat, personable person with a pleasant appearance. Threes do not expend their energy on intimate personal relationships but instead are goal-oriented, future-oriented and work-oriented.

Driven to succeed, they are competitive, hard working and intensely focused on their goals. They are flexible and able to respond creatively to changing circumstances or unexpected problems. Threes quickly become impatient and/or intolerant of people who are pessimistic, who don't follow through on their commitments, or who require detailed instructions. Threes are caught in the feeling of failure and are trying to avoid it by feeling competent, confident and capable.

Positive descriptors. Organized, optimistic, self-assured, efficient, competent, productive, accomplished, adaptable, enthusiastic, decisive, motivators, good communicators.

Negative descriptors. Calculating, self-promoting, opportunistic, deceptive, intolerant, fast-paced, secretive, impatient, political, cold, workaholics, emotional chameleons.

Checklist

If you are a Three, it's likely that you:

☐ Have a talent and a need for accomplishment.

☐ Feel challenged by any task you choose.

☐ Always have a list of your goals, either written or mental.

☐ Are personable and know how to convince people to cooperate with you and with each other to accomplish a goal.

☐ Depend on your ability to put aside your true responses and be what you feel other people expect you to be.

☐ Know how to present yourself in a positive light but can be an internal pessimist when it comes to your own self-esteem.

☐ Are a free thinker who doesn't pay homage to other people, no matter how important, erudite or celebrated they may be.

☐ Can create a positive attitude that energizes entire groups.

☐ Dislike negative talk or "bad attitude" because you feel that pessimism drags everyone down and blocks the creative force necessary to keep moving forward.

☐ Are motivated by rewards, so if you rest on your laurels for any length of time, you find yourself asking, "Is this all there is?"

☐ Can descend into self-pity or depression that may express itself as anger when you feel caught in circumstances that prevent you from achieving.

☐ Meet criticism of you or your work with a strong and well-worded response.

What's Going On Inside

Center configuration. Threes see the world through the feeling center but then don't use that intelligence to process information. Because they *interpret* life through the feeling center, they are aware of emotions (mostly in others but also in themselves) of interpersonal dynamics, and of how they come across to others. But then they *process* that information with the thinking and doing centers, which focuses their attention on their own ideas and actions. Because the feeling center is repressed and not used when they are making sense of the world, their interest in relationships and emotions is often

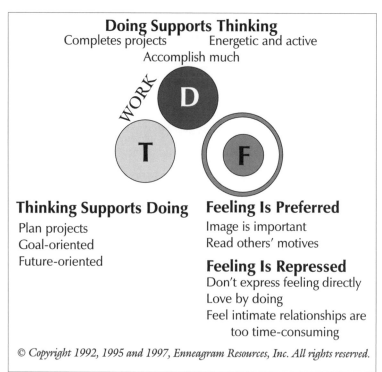

Doing Supports Thinking
Completes projects   Energetic and active
Accomplish much

WORK   D

T   F

Thinking Supports Doing
Plan projects
Goal-oriented
Future-oriented

Feeling Is Preferred
Image is important
Read others' motives

Feeling Is Repressed
Don't express feeling directly
Love by doing
Feel intimate relationships are
          too time-consuming

superficial. Thus, they mechanically respond to the world by gauging their words and actions to elicit the most positive response from others.

Preferred center. The preferred center of intelligence for Threes is the feeling center. Thus, many of the more external qualities of the feeling center are easily accessible to them. Their image of success and the ability to present a pleasant appearance of both social and professional charm is not only natural but vitally important to them. Their political astuteness and professional success is due in large part to the feeling center's capacity to be aware of and respond to other people's feelings, needs, expectations and motives. Being able to communicate and get along with the great majority of people is an asset that rises out of the feeling center.

Support centers and dominant center. The true strengths and abilities of type Three are drawn from the thinking and doing centers of intelligence. Nothing in nature grows perfectly symmetrical; this is also true for the centers of intelligence. Either thinking or doing is dominant in a Three's personality. Yet, qualities of both centers are evident and act together to orient them towards work. Work calls on their abilities both to plan projects (thinking) and to complete projects (doing). Their lives are guided by their expertise in setting both short- and long-range goals (thinking), which they consistently accomplish (doing).

Repressed center. The true purpose of the feeling center is repressed in Threes. This results in being outwardly personable while inwardly distant and impersonal. Valuing clear goals, competency, efficiency and productivity (thinking and doing), they find intimate relationships too time-consuming and quickly become bored and impatient with the expression of feeling in others. Even when Threes are aware of their own feelings, they will rarely share them with others; their experience is that this kind of vulnerability can be used against them at a later time. Thus, work, success, and attaining the admiration of others become their primary life values.

First Steps in Soul Development

When Threes understand the major themes of their personality arise from the thinking and doing centers playing off each other, the first steps to alleviate their compulsions become clear. Separate these two centers so each is developed without the agenda of the other one in view.

Specifically, use the thinking center to ponder the meaning of life, develop creative ideas that contribute to the wellbeing of others, and revive the love of learning. Allow the doing center to stop the hectic schedule and experience the joy of life, relaxation and being.

Finally, it's important to develop the feeling center for its true purposes. Becoming emotionally vulnerable, spending time being with others while giving them their full attention, and appreciating time alone open Threes to the new horizons of valuing themselves as persons and discovering their souls.

Expression of balance. When Threes move forward in the

process of transformation, they display the quality of integrity.

The Formula for the Passion of Deceit

Preferred feeling in Threes says that love and relationships are important. Repressed feeling makes love and relationships seem unreal or impossible. What else can they do but pretend? The result of this internal conflict can only be deceit.

Therefore, Threes' prime values become success, and the image and admiration that accompanies success. Because Threes do not allow themselves to become emotionally connected to other people, their attitude that "anything goes" on their way to the top is laced with deception. Deceit is fueled by the thinking and doing centers playing off each other, causing Threes to believe the impersonal realm is more important than the personal realm.

Core Strengths

► Threes' leadership skills are based on a creative vision for the future and stating clear goals, job descriptions and standards.

► Their optimistic and enthusiastic energy motivates others to work as a unified team to accomplish goals or complete projects.

► A pleasant appearance, ability to communicate, and the capacity to work hard inspires others to have confidence in them, their product or their organization.

81

- Their ability to adapt quickly and efficiently to changing circumstances allows them to achieve their goals in the midst of external difficulties.
- An innate awareness of the feelings, needs and expectations of others makes them politically astute and socially charming.
- They are able to set aside personal offenses or slights and work in harmony to achieve common goals.

Potential Obstacles

- Their inclination to pour excessive time and energy into work can make them vulnerable to the deterioration of their physical health and personal relationships.
- Being deeply invested in their idealized self-image causes them to overlook, ignore or diminish the contributions of others.
- Rather than acknowledging failures and learning from them, Threes tend to ignore failures, deny them, or twist the facts in a way that will make them look like successes.
- They are able to become what they think others want them to be, and to convince themselves and others the image they present is who they really are.
- They may become so focused on achieving the goal that they rationalize themselves into believing "the end justifies the means."
- Their over-identification with the external world of image and success causes them to lose contact with the inner

self, resulting in the belief that life has no meaning beyond itself.

Ways to Develop Relationships and Spiritual Vitality

▶ Respect, acknowledge and give credit to others for their contributions.

▶ Become aware of why and how you take on the image of the person you think others expect you to be; honest recognition is a first step in breaking unconscious patterns that deceive both yourself and others.

▶ Create time to get in touch with and name your own feelings and needs, then share them with your partner, a family member or friend.

▶ Work and projects quickly put you on automatic pilot and consume all your energy. To assist you in breaking that habitual stance, redefine your goals monthly using such criteria as: "Do my goals reflect my deeper values?" "Are they enhancing or undermining my relationship with myself and others?" "Do my goals allow me to remain free to express my creativity and enthusiasm?" "Do my goals require such focused concentration that I am prevented from being open to new or unexpected possibilities?"

▶ Give responsibilities to someone else when you start thinking you are the only one who can do them justice.

▶ Practice patience with, and acceptance of, the idiosyncracies of others.

▶ Be present in the moment and listen to others when they

share their feelings. This means resisting your natural inclination to go mentally AWOL while continuing to wear a mask of genuine interest.

➤ Make time every day to meditate and reflect on the meaning of your life.

➤ Be grateful daily for the dreams you've had that have been fulfilled and for the dreams you never thought of dreaming that you received as pure gift.

Wound

The wound in Threes is emotional isolation/alienation. Thus, the most damage has taken place in the feeling center of intelligence, which consequently has been repressed. As children, Threes learned or came to believe their self-worth depended on what they could do rather than who they are. Looking good, making the family look good, high standards of performance, and being the way other people wanted them to be were rewarded.

Feeling emotionally isolated, Threes quickly distance themselves emotionally from others. Early in life, they determined that expressing feelings is like stepping into quicksand. The only way to stay out of trouble is never to allow their faces to show what is really going on inside. After consistently practicing this exterior deception, eventually Threes lose contact with what goes on inside them. As one Three said upon learning he was not in touch with his feelings, "If my feelings have a hard time getting in touch with me, that's their problem!"

Threes conclude that the way to survive and remain safe is to focus on work and achieve their goals. They don't pin their dreams to anyone else's coattails. Threes can appear so personable that others seldom realize, until after the fact, they were being used to achieve the Three's goals, and now the Three has moved on.

Thus, personal plans, ideas, goals and objectives (thinking center) along with efficiency, productivity and hard work (doing center) become the values around which they build their lives. This illusion of what is important in life perpetuates their original wound of isolation as they continue to emotionally separate from themselves and others.

Repressed Virtue

Of the three great virtues — faith, hope and love — needed for healing and wholeness, Threes have lost the virtue of love. They have lost touch with their capacity to love both themselves and others.

Love flows from the heart — from feeling, relatedness and emotional connectedness. Threes attempt to compensate for the repressed feeling center by overusing the thinking and doing intelligences. They indirectly express the love they feel but cannot articulate verbally. First they think about how they can support the people they love, then do whatever is necessary to give them what they need.

Attempting to express love solely through recognition

and action deprives them of the fullness of love. Until the emotionally vulnerable and expressive part of them awakens and reclaims its rightful place in their lives, fulfilling relationships and spiritual vitality elude them. This can happen only through spending time in reflection, prayer, meditation, putting a priority on time for sharing feelings with other people, and spending time in artistic creation. After expending energy in these ways, a yearning stirred by dim memories of something higher will lead them to the truth of who they really are. Then, with the mysteries of love awakened, their souls will find a home and flourish in the Source of love.

Forgotten Child

Threes' forgotten child is the loving, spiritual, gentle child who finds its home in the heart. Because the heart has been wounded, this child has not been nourished to grow to its full potential. Threes, who were rewarded for looking good and being winners, came to believe their worth depended on what they could accomplish, not on being who they are and living in their souls.

Being what others expected, playing a role, and looking good on the outside no matter what was happening on the inside was far safer than being emotionally vulnerable. Talking about or acting on their feelings exposed them to being misunderstood, being the brunt of laughter or, even worse, getting into trouble.

To reclaim the beauty and gifts embodied in this forgotten

part of themselves, Threes need to lighten up on their work load and slow down the pace of their lives. "Wasting" time on relationships, meditation, art, and watching the clouds float by yield the lost treasure in their lives.

Orientation to Time

Threes' future orientation is directly connected to their lost virtue of love. You do not have to love what does not yet exist. No matter what goal they finally achieve, there is no sense of satisfaction unless and until they have their eyes on the next goal. Without interrupting this compulsively forward-focused pattern, Threes not only miss the love and joy that can only be found in the present moment, but they also unconsciously and mechanically create a loveless future.

Challenge

The most important quest for Threes is to become personal as well as personable, to become truly relational rather than to use relationships to further their own goals. By dismissing the importance of the feeling center and thus of the personal realm, Threes believe they are free to use their doing and thinking centers in tandem without restraint. The thinking center creates the plan and the doing center accomplishes it. This is the origin of their focus on work, achievement and success so that others will admire them.

Threes need to slow down, first to experience their emotions, and finally to experience their real selves or souls.

At first, they will only do this in time spent alone and away from work. Since it's almost unheard of for Threes to be doing nothing, journal writing or artistic pursuits promote personal reflection.

With a more interior orientation of quiet and meditation, they learn to discern what is good for their own soul and pursue it with dedication. They come to value rest and relaxation as ways to explore the realms of the soul, knowing a latent philosopher or romantic may well emerge. Having discovered their inner life, they are able to share it with others. They not only discover the fulfillment of loving and being loved in relationships, they also come to know and love themselves as human beings.

Summary of Type Three

Avoidance. Failure.

Passion. Deceit.

Preferred center. Feeling.

Dominant center. Doing or Thinking.

Support center. Thinking or Doing.

Repressed center. Feeling.

Stance. Aggressive.

Orientation to time. Future.

Wound. Emotional isolation/alienation.

Repressed virtue. Love.

Forgotten child. Spiritual, loving, gentle child.

Divine image. Love.

Questions for Reflection for Threes

1. What specific ways do I withhold information, tell half truths, or simply lie to protect my image? What of value do I gain from any of these tactics?

2. Why do I deny others the right to be different from me by forcing my ideas and/or values on them? What am I not understanding about them that I need to understand?

3. Why do I continue to remain silent about things I know in my heart need to be expressed?

4. Which qualities do people close to me verbally or nonverbally ask me to develop, and why do I resist these requests?

5. What are the issues in me I need to face because they prevent me from openly giving credit to others for their contributions?

6. Why do I resist or fear creating the time in my life necessary to awaken my spiritual energy?

7. What meaning or values do I truly want my life to communicate?

FOUR: THE INDIVIDUALIST

Quick Overview

Thumbnail sketch. Fours are emotionally sensitive people who strive for meaning and value in both their relationships and work. Never satisfied with living on the surface, they seek to understand everything at a deeper level. Fours overly identify with their own emotional life and generally are not objective.

Because they are overly analytical, Fours are hyper-aware of what's missing both inside and out. Their refined aesthetic sense gives Fours an extraordinary appreciation of beauty, art and goodness in the world. Fours are caught in a sense of inferiority about themselves and the ordinariness of life. They strive to avoid them by feeling unique.

Positive descriptors. Sensitive, original, charming, insightful, perceptive, aesthetic, relational, authentic, empathetic, clear thinkers, precise teachers, gifted counselors.

Negative descriptors. Self-absorbed, blaming, demanding, dramatic, inhibited, overanalyzing, critical, intense, unfulfilled, moody, misunderstood, easily embarrassed.

Checklist

If you are a Four, it's likely that you:

☐ See the world through a wide range of bright and dark, subtle and dramatic emotions.

☐ Can easily find yourself in a dark mood because the world is a difficult place and it's so hard to get what you want out of life.

☐ Are able to initiate original programs and projects.

☐ Are attracted to any activities or pursuits that stimulate emotion, allow you to express feeling, or combine your native interests in personal expression and relationships.

☐ Have an aversion to mediocrity and therefore love both traditional and off-beat complex things, people and situations.

☐ Seek to understand why other people do what they do and have insight into situations.

☐ Believe the world would be a better place if everyone tried harder to understand themselves and others.

☐ Find it easy both to be contrite for your mistakes and justify your behavior, depending on the situation and the people in it.

☐ Seek to be understood and feel you have the right to it.

☐ Tend either to be quiet or freely divulge personal information, and especially to explain your feelings.

☐ Tend to deal with conflicts with authority by laying all your cards on the table, even though it is difficult to trust everything will turn out all right.

☐ Believe that being an honest and authentic person is an important value most people don't take seriously enough.

What's Going On Inside

Center configuration. Fours see and *interpret* the world through the feeling center so their values include their image, emotions, relationships and interpersonal dynamics. They *make sense* out of life with the feeling and thinking intelligences, which orients their interest to what's going on inside them and others. Having a repressed doing center means they don't feel they can affect their environment; all that is left is their inner world of feeling. They mechanically

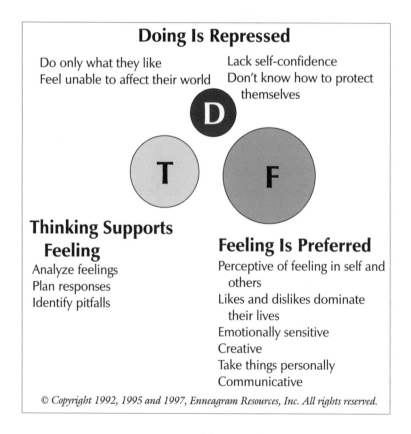

Doing Is Repressed

Do only what they like
Feel unable to affect their world

Lack self-confidence
Don't know how to protect
 themselves

Thinking Supports Feeling

Analyze feelings
Plan responses
Identify pitfalls

Feeling Is Preferred

Perceptive of feeling in self and
 others
Likes and dislikes dominate
 their lives
Emotionally sensitive
Creative
Take things personally
Communicative

respond to the world by taking life personally and ruminating on its many implications.

Preferred center and dominant center. Fours, in whom the feeling center is both preferred and dominant, derive their prime sense of meaning and fulfillment through their relationships. Their emotional sensitivity, which is both a strength and a stumbling block, fuels a deep longing for something or someone to make them feel whole. The inward focus of the feeling center makes them intensely aware of their own likes, dislikes and desires. Often charming, they are able to respond to problems, pain and suffering with compassion, insight and understanding.

Support center. With the thinking center supporting the feeling center, Fours' emotional sensitivities are focused inward. They automatically analyze both their own and others' feelings. Gaining insight and understanding into why and how they developed into the person they are is important to Fours. Their minds race ahead, spontaneously responding to future problems or disputes. Thinking supporting feeling creates a fertile imagination, critical thinking skills and a curiosity that allow Fours to internally question everything until they finally understand.

Repressed center. Fours' discomfort with and tendency to ignore the practical and mundane realities of everyday life is the result of having a repressed doing intelligence. It isn't that they don't do anything. Rather, they fritter away their time doing whatever makes them feel good. Meanwhile, tasks like mowing the yard, balancing the checkbook or cleaning the house are either left undone or left for someone else to do. Doing center qualities like stamina, determination, self-assurance and self-confidence are generally unavailable to compulsive Fours. Until these gifts are developed they lament, complain and feel like victims of circumstance.

First Steps in Soul Development

When Fours realize the feeling-thinking center team creates all the illusions that cause them difficulty, they can begin to deal effectively with the situation. Reclaiming true personhood for type Four begins in separating the feeling and thinking centers so that each can achieve its own true purpose. Instead of only using qualities from the thinking center that support the feeling center's agenda, they use thinking to gain objectivity, plan their day, attend to details, and be curious about what others need. They also learn to use their feeling center to connect them creatively with other people, the universe and Spirit, not just to experience their own emotional life.

Then, the best place to focus their attention is on the doing center. Though frightening at first, the strength and energy of this center soon become exciting; Fours realize that opening it is the pathway to the joy of accomplishment and achievement. Fours enhance their lives by placing doing what needs to be done ahead of doing what pleases them. They learn to think practically by looking ahead to the consequences of their words and actions, by taking all details into account as they estimate the time it takes to accomplish a task, and by taking responsibility for the mundane and distasteful tasks of life.

This work allows them to discover the place within from which they can state their needs directly. They are able to appropriately confront situations that frighten them. As determination, drive and accomplishment take their place in Fours' lives, hope grows. The joy of being alive, which is innate to the doing center, is the best antidote to the pessimism and envy that arise when they overvalue their feelings.

Expression of balance. As Fours travel down the path of transformation, they become serene.

Formula for the Passion of Envy

The preferred/dominant feeling center in Fours causes them to place their prime value on feelings and relationships. Their support thinking center continually ruminates on how they feel about themselves and compares themselves to the people they admire. Repressed doing means they have lost touch with the ability to affect their environment and get what they want and need. What else is left for them but envy?

Fours easily recognize others' strengths and good fortune while, in comparison, their own talents seem insignificant. Discontent because they are aware of what is missing from their lives, they feel ordinary at best and inferior at worst.

Core Strengths

➤ Fours' leadership is grounded in honest and respectful communication and achieving excellence without compromising quality or deeper values.

➤ Boredom with complacent routine ignites their creative energy and causes them to rise above the ordinary to strive to be the best in their field.

➤ They have an innate emotional sensitivity to and genuine concern for each individual in a family, community or organization.

➤ Their ability to identify potential problems prepares them to respond quickly when and if difficulties arise down the road.

➤ Fours recognize the beauty in people and nature that is often missed by others.

➤ Able to listen, understand and synthesize the information they receive, Fours can become insightful teachers, counselors, therapists and spiritual directors.

Potential Obstacles

➤ Continually focusing on what's missing in their lives prevents Fours from recognizing their own gifts or being grateful for their good fortune.

➤ Their tendency to take everything personally and become upset when obstacles arise lead to blaming and finding fault with others.

➤ Emotional explosions or moodiness can cause others to

view them as unstable.

➤ Finding fault and imagining future difficulties when new projects are proposed can encourage others to view them as pessimistic, negative and difficult to work with or be around.

➤ Being too open about how they feel and/or about their private lives often creates difficulties for them at a later time.

➤ Lacking confidence to deal with the world of practical things, Fours can create resentment in others by manipulating and overburdening them with their neediness.

Ways to Develop Relationships and Spiritual Vitality

➤ Become aware of what causes your emotional temperature to go up or down. Interrupt these patterns before the intensity controls you; for example, take a walk or weed the garden.

➤ Resist the impulse to criticize a new idea or a person you don't understand. Instead, remain silent, say something positive, or look at it from the other person's point of view.

➤ When a task seems overwhelming or when you simply dislike it, remember it still needs to be done. As one Four said, "I just tell myself, 'Think and do, think and do. It doesn't matter how I feel. Think and do.' Finally it's done."

➤ Notice what your partner, friend or co-worker values or needs and respond without being asked.

➤ Identify your own talents and accept them without bragging about them. This will keep you from envying others and provide a stable platform for all the other parts of your life.

➤ When you find that special relationship, cherish it, nurture it, pour all your energy, enthusiasm, creativity and love into it.

➤ Identify the patterns of speech by which you draw others' attention to yourself. When you notice them in conversations, refocus the topic onto another person.

➤ Instead of rehashing the hurts from your past, clearly identify what your experience was, find healing and resolution for those painful times, and let them go.

Wound

The wound that most injured Fours, causing them to repress their doing intelligence, is emotional and/or physical abandonment. As children, Fours came to believe they were abandoned because something was wrong with them, but they didn't know what it was. This gnawing awareness led to a lack of self-confidence and a growing appreciation of and desire for the strong, wonderful things they saw in others. They felt they were growing up emotionally alone, without guidance. Feeling inferior and insecure, they attempted to become unique so that others would love them so much that they could never leave them again.

They also examined the behavior and feelings of others.

Wanting to understand themselves and others grew out of a yearning to find someone who would understand and love them. Out of this attitude flows their intense need for relationship and connection. Believing they are unlovable and can't depend on others, Fours continue to perpetuate the pain of abandonment by developing close relationships, then testing them until they push the other person away.

Healing this wound begins when Fours get out of their thoughts and feelings and start taking their share of responsibility in the practical world of daily life. Regarding meditation, they are so at home in the inner world, they often do best with practices like walking meditation and body disciplines. Their inward focus needs to be drawn outward to achieve balance. Sweat, the sweet fragrance of physical work — cleaning the house, mowing the lawn, painting a room — invigorates the low doing center energy and authenticates the soul.

Repressed Virtue

Having lost contact with one of the three great virtues, hope, Fours substitute many "little hopes" to help them get through life. When they discovered they couldn't count on anyone, hope shriveled to what they themselves could imagine. Thus, they call their fantasies hope. Without real hope, pessimism reigns. It fuels despair, self-pity, self-doubt, feelings of inferiority, and the sense something is seriously wrong with them and their lives.

Brother David Steindl-Rast described the virtue of hope

as the freedom to be "open to surprise." Compulsive Fours need to be prepared ahead of time for any real or imagined problems. Their need to script conversations in various ways before they ever occur, resistance to new projects or ideas, and pessimistic attitudes result from losing the virtue of hope. Openness to surprise requires a kind of courage not readily available to them.

When Fours begin to release their grip on the inner world and learn to honor and accept the unpredictability of the outer world, they relax into the promise-filled realm of the unknown. As they learn to love the physical universe, hope leads them toward the greatest mystery of all — intimate union with the Source of all belonging.

Forgotten Child

The adventuresome, spontaneous, playful child was dismissed, silenced and forgotten in Fours. This child is the container and keeper of wonder, joy and surprise — the foundation on which hope securely rests. Love, sensitivity, questioning and curiosity moved forward to assist Fours in feeling safe in the world.

Awakening and embracing these naturally confident and gregarious aspects of themselves will happen each time they acknowledge and express gratitude for the gifts and strengths they've developed throughout life. They reduce self-absorption by learning to recognize others, trusting they can work through difficulties when they arise, not allowing moods to determine their attitude for the day, and accepting respon-sibility for mundane as well as glorious tasks. These ways help reclaim the power and energy of the adventuresome child within who will guide them to their souls.

Orientation to Time

Dwelling on the past and longing for "what could have been" overshadows the lives of Fours, preventing them from recognizing they are missing the virtue of hope. Staying locked in the past reinforces their defenses against being caught off balance by the unexpected. With this attitude they can justify their belief that others should treat them with kid gloves by not bringing up anything difficult in the evening, new in the morning, or spontaneous in the afternoon.

As Fours resolve the pain of past abandonment, they discover the wonder, surprise and hope contained in the present moment. With this foundation they can imagine and create a happy future.

Challenge

The most important quest for Fours is to take charge of their lives and cease living as victims of the forces around them. Fours' hyper-awareness of their own inner lives — the result of the feeling center being supported by the analytical thinking center — rivets their attention on what's missing and what's wrong for them. These two centers overwhelm the doing center, so it cannot bring to bear its vitality, power and joy. All they're left with is a consuming envy for those who have what they feel missing in themselves.

The most life-giving discipline for Fours is to surrender feeling that something is seriously wrong with their lives, abandon their envious desires, and place their lives in the service of the will of the higher self. Through regular meditation they learn to sort through their emotions, gain perspective over their problems, and deepen their intuitions and perceptions of Truth. Grounded in reality, their practical assessment of their situation frees them to activate the power necessary to creatively give direction to their own lives. Through connecting their souls to a higher Source, Fours cease resisting change and their victim mentality fades.

Summary of Type Four

Avoidance. Inferiority.

Passion. Envy.

Preferred center. Feeling.

Dominant center. Feeling.

Support center. Thinking.

Repressed center. Doing.

Stance. Withdrawing.

Orientation to time. Past.

Wound. Abandonment.

Repressed virtue. Hope.

Forgotten child. Adventuresome, spontaneous, playful child.

Divine image. Power.

Questions for Reflection for Fours

1. What specific projects have I been avoiding, and how would it benefit me and others if I completed them?
2. What are the detrimental effects to my relationships caused by my failure to take my share of day-to-day responsibilities?
3. When I push away someone I care about, what am I really saying, and how can I resolve the underlying issue?
4. Who in my life do I most try to manipulate and/or control by bringing up past offenses and why?
5. What are five strengths or talents I have developed in my life, and am I using them effectively?
6. How could I creatively put my strengths forward in the material world in a way that would most increase my self-confidence and monetary compensation without compromising my values?
7. What are ten gifts an adventuresome, spontaneous, playful child might develop in a healthy way to make life happy and to contribute to society?

FIVE: THE OBSERVER

Quick Overview

Thumbnail sketch. Fives are independent thinkers who value planning, knowledge, concepts and ideas. They are perceptive, patient and insightful listeners, a quality that is enhanced by their inner non-attachment to people and life. Analysis, theory, research and synthesizing information are strengths that allow them to sift out the nonessential elements and pierce through to the heart of what is important. They intellectualize life and often speak of it as if they are not a part of it.

Fives are nonconformists who create an eccentric image that secretly amuses them. It also excuses them from having to be tactful in their speech or develop social skills they find boring. They are clear, concise communicators who are often recognized experts in their field. Their exaggerated need for privacy leads them to become self-reliant, resourceful and self-motivated. Fives are caught in a feeling of emptiness; they try to avoid this feeling by being full of knowledge.

Positive descriptors. Observant, thoughtful, attentive, perceptive, informed, concise, deliberate, curious, discerning, logical, humorous, knowledgeable.

Negative descriptors. Uninvolved, superior, distant, tactless, reclusive, hoarding, cold, independent, intolerant, contemptuous, sarcastic, anti-social.

Checklist

If you are a Five, it's likely that you:

☐ Like to stand back and take a long, cool look before you draw conclusions or make decisions.

☐ Don't like feelings to get in the way of logic.

☐ Notice the quirks in life and people and use dry humor to comment on them.

☐ Express your commitment to and love for others by sharing your ideas with them.

☐ Enjoy piercing to the core of an issue and understanding it.

☐ Are known for being both consistent and persistent in expressing your ideas.

☐ Generally don't say anything unless you have something important to say.

☐ Wonder why other people say so many things that don't need to be said, repeat themselves, and go off the topic.

☐ Find that other people usually don't understand your ideas.

☐ Tend to leave social overtures to the other party and social arrangements to your partner or best friend.

☐ Find small talk boring and avoid situations in which you may be required to create it.

☐ Need little by way of "creature comforts" except in one or two areas in which you often indulge yourself.

What's Going On Inside

Center configuration. Fives see and *interpret* the world through the thinking center and therefore value information, logic and discovering patterns. They *process* information with thinking and feeling, which orients their interest toward what's going on inside them. Inasmuch as their doing center is repressed, they don't feel they can affect their environment, so all that is left is their ideas. They mechanically respond to life by defending their ideas because they feel so deeply about them.

Preferred center and dominant center. Fives' pre-

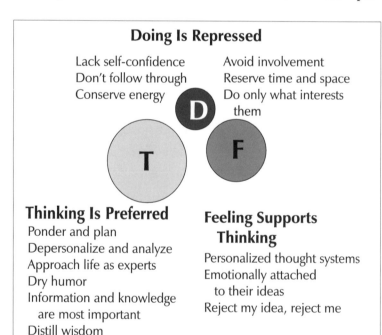

Doing Is Repressed

Lack self-confidence
Don't follow through
Conserve energy

Avoid involvement
Reserve time and space
Do only what interests
   them

Thinking Is Preferred
Ponder and plan
Depersonalize and analyze
Approach life as experts
Dry humor
Information and knowledge
   are most important
Distill wisdom

**Feeling Supports
   Thinking**
Personalized thought systems
Emotionally attached
   to their ideas
Reject my idea, reject me

ferred/dominant thinking center is the basis for their being most at home in the inner world of ideas, observations and logic. The outer world is primarily an interesting place to gather information. Fives approach life as dispassionate intellectual experts and depend on their dry sense of humor to help them connect with a social world in which they feel uncomfortable. Fives can become so invested in their own perceptions and ideas that they may be unwilling to even consider the insights and contributions of others. When other people propose ideas different from theirs, they can easily object, disagree or oppose. They may also take the superior stance of dismissing the idea as irrelevant, saying the other person's thought is a part of the idea they are proposing, or simply remain silent.

Support center. Feeling supports thinking, which means that for Fives, knowledge is always a personalized reality. It's not just knowledge, it's *their* knowledge. They are as identified with what they know as Fours are with how they feel. Fives are always their own philosophers, psychologists, theologians, etc. Because they enjoy being known for their originality and unusual perspectives, they feel personally hurt and rejected when their ideas are not valued or understood. Because Fives use the feeling intelligence to support their thinking, the energies of emotion and passion are attached to their ideas. This leaves little feeling energy to spend relating emotionally with others. When asked what his greatest difficulty in life was, one Five answered, "People. They're such a mystery!" To

Fives, people are unpredictable and all too often uninteresting.

Repressed center. The repressed doing center in Fives becomes obvious in the way they conserve their energy and avoid involvement in life. They guard and protect their privacy so as not to become bogged down in unpleasant everyday entanglements. They give away their time and energy — even to people whom they love — only if they decide there is a valid reason. Lacking the self-confidence that is a natural strength of the doing intelligence, Fives severely restrict to the absolute essential the time they spend at social functions or in meetings. Fives invest a great deal of time and energy in doing what interests them, while they can ignore or do not see tasks that objectively need to be done. They love to plan, refine their plans, and rethink the details over and over again. However, in their personal lives, their plans may not get off the drawing board unless someone else pushes them to start the project.

First Steps in Soul Development

The team of the thinking center (ideas) supported by feeling (personal emotional ownership) creates the illusion that life is about developing and refining personalized belief systems. The discovery of true personhood for Fives begins in separating the thinking and feeling centers so each can achieve its own true purpose. All that Fives know about their feeling center is what the thinking center draws from it to support its agenda.

When the two centers are released from their lockstep position, the thinking center can be used for creative, flexible thinking, pondering the meaning of life, and openness to other people's ideas. The feeling center is then free to be properly used for connecting with people, resolving personal conflicts, and relating emotionally with the universe and with the divine. This movement creates space for the energy of the doing center to emerge in their lives.

To achieve balance and harmony, Fives need to develop and value the doing intelligence for its true purposes. As Fives become more action-oriented, their egocentric investment in their ideas diminishes. They move beyond the planning stage to discover the exhilaration that comes with accomplishment. They learn to think practically and plan their projects with more accurate estimates of the time, money and materials they will require. They also develop projects that influence the material world in a practical way. This work allows the lighter, more spontaneous and playful gifts of the doing center to emerge. In the balancing of centers, they discover the potential of their souls.

Expression of balance. As Fives move forward toward the goal of transformation, they become generous.

Formula for the Passion of Greed

The passion driving the Five personality is greed — not necessarily for money, but for time and space to think, plan, develop their pet theories, or work on projects that interest them. Their preferred thinking center causes them to value knowledge, information and ideas. The thinking center turns outward to the world to compensate for the repressed doing center, which normally relates a person to the world. With their feeling center supporting the thinking center, an insatiable desire to learn everything possible drives them. Thus, greed for knowledge dominates their lives. Secretive, Fives never reveal all they know, rarely disclose where they stand on any issue until the final moment, and are loath to divulge any information about their private lives.

Core Strengths

▶ Leadership based on thorough planning, clear strategy, vision and a detailed action plan prepares them to delegate day-to-day responsibilities to people who can carry the plan forward and can also compensate for their own lack of interpersonal skills.

▶ Outstanding abilities to consolidate information and communicate in clear, concise terms clarifies expectations and eliminates confusion.

▶ Personal detachment is an asset that enables them to evaluate difficulties without emotional bias and perceive the salient issues that need to be addressed.

▶ Perceptive listening skills make them good mediators who are able to help others understand the meaning of their own experience.

▶ They promote growth and change because they can present new ideas in logical terms with cleverness and humor.

▶ They possess an irrepressible curiosity about and appreciation for life.

Potential Obstacles

▶ A proclivity for observing life can prevent them from experiencing the joy of living their own lives.

▶ Unreasonable needs for privacy, both spacial and psychological, can lead to becoming isolated not only from others but also from themselves.

▶ A propensity for emotional detachment and barking orders from behind the "wizard's curtain" can cause others to feel demeaned and manipulated by remote control.

▶ Using logic to try to resolve relational difficulties magnifies their superior attitude and increases the intensity of conflicts.

▶ Their tendency to ignore and failure to communicate their needs leave others without the information needed to support them.

▶ Forgetting that other people in their lives are motivated by relational connections may deny them the support and networking needed to achieve their dreams and possibilities.

111

Ways to Develop Relationships and Spiritual Vitality

► Include and respect the personal interactions and connections that are primary values to others.

► Learn to compromise on issues that don't impact your personal values.

► Honor with understanding the fears of others when sudden change and difficulties arise.

► Because others are aware you value your time alone, make sure you communicate directly with them, let them know specifically how they can support you, and tell them when you will be available.

► Remember to verbally acknowledge and appreciate others for who they are and what they contribute. Expecting they should automatically know what they mean to you is interpreted as being thoughtless and passive-aggressive.

► Become aware of the times you withdraw both mentally and physically. Once you can recognize and name the discomfort internally, clearly communicate what you need from other people to help you remain present.

► Get up, get out and volunteer your services to a worthwhile cause — for example, Habitat for Humanity, a soup kitchen or a local family in need — because activity energizes the doing intelligence.

► Use ritual to connect your inner experience with physical reality.

Wound

Abandonment, whether emotional or physical, is the core wound in Fives, and it led to withdrawing into the thinking center. Whenever life became difficult, Fives could escape into their own invisible world where they felt safe, had some control, and pursued their own interests. They could think whatever they wanted or imagine traveling to far distant lands without getting in trouble or being criticized for saying or doing the wrong thing.

The physical world feels dangerous and unpredictable when your doing center has receded into the background. Without the gifts of that intelligence, Fives lose the self-confidence and hope they need to believe they can survive in or change their external reality. Nearly invisible because of their taciturn nature, Fives peer into the world, observe, and gather the information that fascinates them. Then they bring it back into the safety of their own minds to analyze and understand. Even Fives who have learned how to be more social have said, "No one knows how hard it is for me to do this. I crave time alone."

Having lost confidence in the safety and wholeness of life, Fives turned inward. Thus, venturing into the unfamiliar "Mad, Mad World" of physical reality and interpersonal exchange is the risky and exciting exploration that will heal the wound and allow Fives ". . . to arrive where (they) started/ And know the place for the first time" (T. S. Eliot, *Four Quartets*").

Repressed Virtue

Fives' early life history of physical and/or emotional desertion devastated their self-perception and left them feeling personally hopeless. They can access and develop the virtues of faith and love, but even these become distorted without the third great virtue that remains repressed and unavailable to them — hope.

The lack of hope, described by David Steindl-Rast as an openness to surprise, is visible in Fives in their demand to have everything predictable. They want time to prepare so they know they won't be caught off guard. The spontaneity of the doing center is reduced to knee-jerk reactions followed by quick retreats. Since there is no way to be prepared for unexpected interactions, Fives say as little as possible.

Detachment, a distinct aspect of Fives' compulsion, creates the illusion both for themselves and for others that they are objective. Pleased by this development, they view it as a virtue rather than the obstacle of indifference that it actually is. As they accept this truth, they glimpse the vision of harmony and beauty that blends inner and outer worlds into a cohesive whole. By developing freedom to move between inner and outer reality, a passion for the possible is born and soul is reunited with the Source, the origin of all hope.

Forgotten Child

The need for predictability, planning, information and distance all came forward as the adventuresome, spontaneous, playful child that lives in the doing intelligence was forgotten. Without the wild and free gifts that this child possesses, Fives retreat to a safer, more secure, controlled and controllable environment.

To reclaim the gifts and freedom of this child who explodes with wild abandon, Fives cannot tiptoe or whisper their invitation. They must knock down the doors and shout their welcome from the housetops! At least that is the way it will feel to the reserved, self-protective Five. The point is that internal perceptions or awareness, like a horn without a mouthpiece, will never be loud enough to awaken this child. Only action and emotional engagement will awaken this energy that gives life to the soul. Then training this child will require stamina, discipline and determination.

Orientation to Time

Fives compensate for their insecurities in dealing with the physical and interpersonal dimensions of life and the loss of hope by focusing on the past. Uncertain of where and how they fit in, they dwell on analyzing knowledge, information already gained and past experiences in an attempt to reach an objective understanding of life. You are protected from both the dangers of the present and the pressures of the future if you remain focused on the past. This attitude protects Fives from recognizing their lack of hope and from the pain of their original wound of abandonment.

Challenge

The most important quest for Fives is to connect personally with the real world and test their ideas in it. Because their feeling center supports the thinking center, they personalize and cling to their own ideas, their own point of view. The depth of feeling they have about their ideas creates rigid beliefs and a stubborn defense of their own way of doing things. Their repressed doing center only adds to the problem because it causes a discomfort with accomplishment and a lack of natural assertiveness that makes them cling to their ideas all the more.

Thus, their lives are greatly enhanced by balancing their rich mental world with living, relating and accomplishing in the real world. It's not only a matter of becoming active, but also of engaging emotionally with others, revealing their private inner world of feeling, and receiving others at the feeling level. When all three centers are free to be used appropriately, truth, goodness and beauty (the values of the soul) flourish and create a profound respect for all of life.

Summary of Type Five

Avoidance. Emptiness.

Passion. Avarice/Greed.

Preferred center. Thinking.

Dominant center. Thinking.

Support center. Feeling.

Repressed center. Doing.

Stance. Withdrawing.

Orientation to time. Past.

Wound. Abandonment.

Repressed virtue. Hope.

Forgotten child. Adventuresome, spontaneous, playful child.

Divine image. Beauty.

Questions for Reflection for Fives

1. What prevents me from clearly thinking through the hurtful or embarrassing effects my tactless comments have on others, and how could I change that pattern?

2. What circumstances make me most uncomfortable in the practical physical world, and what could I do or learn to help neutralize that discomfort?

3. How does leaving social responsibilities and initiatives to other people undermine my relationship with myself and with others?

4. What are the issues in me that I need to resolve because they prevent me from emotionally connecting with others?

5. When I control, manipulate and frustrate others by retreating into silence rather than dealing with issues, what of lasting value do I (or anyone else) gain?

6. What are the ways I use superiority and inflexibility to intimidate others and protect myself from changing?

7. What values would I like my family, friends and acquaintances to remember me for?

Six: The Guardian

Quick Overview

Thumbnail sketch. Sixes are responsible people who are driven in their highly active lives by an underlying sense of mistrust as well as a desire to be included. Sociably, graciously, they express their needs as desires for personal interaction. Needing connection with people who are important to them, their family and/or a primary reference group become the recipients of their dedication and loyalty.

They are information-oriented people who often ask what seems to others to be impertinent questions. They idealize team cooperation to counteract their indecisiveness. Caught in apprehension and wanting to avoid it, they desire to feel secure.

Positive descriptors. Responsible, loyal, energetic, hospitable, dedicated, enthusiastic, socially charming, stable, reliable, law-abiding, dependable, networkers.

Negative descriptors. Overinvolved, indecisive, unforgiving, dogmatic, legalistic, doubting, hyper-vigilant, worrying, catastrophizing, hesitant, intolerant.

Checklist

If you are a Six, it's likely that you:

☐ Keep a full schedule and enjoy being active.

☐ Like people to tell you that you are performing well and that you are loved, respected and appreciated.

☐ Think the most respectful way to make a decision is to gather the opinions of those who will be affected by it and take this information into account as you make it.

☐ Value the cards, notes and letters people give you and appreciate the gifts people give you as symbols of their respect.

☐ Consider it an element of prudence to gain the appropriate credentials you need to do your job and similarly appreciate others who have achieved credentials for their work.

☐ Like to know the rules, customs or norms in a situation so you can determine the way you want to respond.

☐ Appreciate order, ceremony and protocol, and like having a person or group set these parameters and put them into effect.

☐ Are responsible and wonder why others can be irresponsible.

☐ Sometimes feel you are too responsible and need to strike out on your own and have your own way.

☐ Do your share of the work and wish others would do the same.

☐ Let others know your feelings when they are consistently ungrateful for your hard work, though it may take you a long time to reach the point of saying something.

☐ Appreciate those who support you and make their decisions in the light of the needs of all.

What's Going On Inside

Center configuration. Sixes *interpret* the world through the thinking center but then don't use thinking to *process* or make sense of the information they have received. Preferred thinking focuses their interest on information, analysis and discovering patterns. Then, because they make sense out of life with the feeling and doing centers, they want to respond to the situations life presents to them. However, with the thinking center repressed at the level of processing information, it cannot guide their response, nor can they evaluate

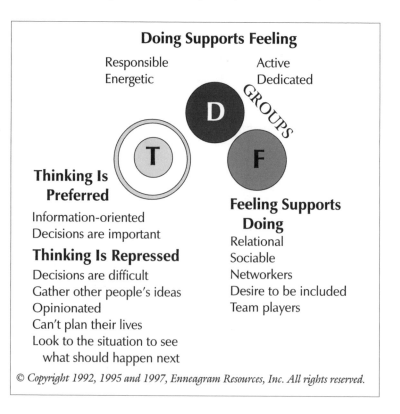

Doing Supports Feeling

Responsible
Energetic

Active
Dedicated

D

GROUPS

T

F

**Thinking Is
   Preferred**

Information-oriented
Decisions are important

Thinking Is Repressed

Decisions are difficult
Gather other people's ideas
Opinionated
Can't plan their lives
Look to the situation to see
   what should happen next

**Feeling Supports
   Doing**

Relational
Sociable
Networkers
Desire to be included
Team players

how well they respond. Repressed thinking causes them to link every issue to every other issue so that they become confused and dismiss the importance of objectivity. They mechanically respond to life by attempting to focus in and be conscientious as they respond to the situation.

Preferred center. In Sixes, the preferred thinking center is the genesis of their need for information. They gather information from everyone but then question whether it is trustworthy. They corroborate the information they have gathered by asking more questions. They also feel a need to schedule their time and organize their day. Having clear rules and standards is essential for them because it relieves their anxiety that things might go wrong.

Support centers and dominant center. Sixes are known for the qualities that arise from the doing and feeling centers. They are responsible people and know the practical steps needed to get a project started. They have the energy and determination to follow the project through to completion. Sixes are also active and productive, and they connect with others through commonly shared experiences. All of these strengths flow from the doing intelligence.

The feeling intelligence allows Sixes to relate with many people; they enjoy connecting people with each other. Sixes, who consistently look to others for support and reassurance, are drawn to groups in every area of their lives — family, community, church and in the business world. They are team players and feel most secure when they know everyone is really committed to the group, when responsibilities are shared, and when there is a free flow of information. They are dedicated, loyal and willing to sacrifice their time and talent for the betterment of family, friends and members of their primary reference groups. Sixes are also known for being gracious, hospitable and socially charming. Either the feeling or the doing center will dominate the way Sixes make sense out of life, and the other center will support the first.

Repressed center. The repressed thinking intelligence in Sixes allows only the most external expressions of the center to be readily available to them. Because they are not in touch with their ability to think for themselves, they need rules and structure to guide them. Sixes cling to the "tried and true" to avoid the insecurity of change. They consistently look to others for the support, reassurance and connection that will alleviate their fear of not being included. Sixes' chronic worrying — having a few facts and filling in the blanks with negative imagination and wrong connections — is a misuse of the thinking center. So is their chronic complaining when things don't go their way or when people disappoint them. Also, being opinionated, stubborn and unforgiving when crossed indicate an underdeveloped thinking intelligence.

First Steps in Soul Development

The movement towards wholeness for Sixes begins in separating the doing center (responsibility) from the feeling center (relatedness) so that each can achieve its true purpose.

Used appropriately, the doing intelligence not only yields productivity, stamina and ease in the practical world; it also frees Sixes from their constant motion. With rest and a renewed sense of the beauty of life, they have time to create things that satisfy and reveal meaning, direction and purpose. Freed, the feeling intelligence is available to express emotion directly, develop intimate relationships, and give rise to compassion through an honest acceptance of others.

Strengthening the repressed thinking center interrupts old patterns. They learn to ponder and sort out the issues in their lives, lose the need to compulsively gather information and depend on reassurance from others to tell them who they are or if they're doing a good job. Instead, they find the courage to connect with and follow their own inner guidance and intuition. They trust their own impressions and therefore are able to make decisions and proceed. They develop an openness to new ideas, new information and new ways of doing things. They think creatively about their lives and plan for the future guided by dreams instead of worries.

Expression of balance. As Sixes move forward in the process of transformation, they become courageous.

Formula for the Passion of Fear

Sixes believe information is important (preferred thinking) but never are sure that they have enough or the right information (repressed thinking). They believe decisions are important but find them difficult to make. Preferring and repressing the thinking intelligence creates fear. The driving passion behind Sixes, fear is often felt as a slight but constant apprehension about life, the future, relationships or their own performance. Fear is the source of their cautiousness, indecisiveness and even their graciousness because, if you can charm people and win their approval, you don't have to fear their response to you.

Core Strengths

▶ Sixes lead through open communication, personal loyalty, clear standards and procedures, easy access to information for everyone, and recognition of individual accomplishment.

▶ They possess a great stamina for work, do not mind overtime, and sacrifice for the greater good of the group.

▶ Sixes' loyalty and wholehearted dedication create atmospheres of comfort and security.

▶ Their social charm, enthusiasm and appreciation of common experience and fun create harmony and balance.

▶ Sixes impart solid values, which permeate the heart of any group to which they are committed.

▶ A respect and honoring of tradition grounds their family, community or institution in the reality of their collective story, history and evolving truth.

Potential Obstacles

▶ Their need for rules and structure can easily devolve into rigid, inflexible standards imposed on others and by which others are judged and even condemned.

▶ Their desires to protect and nurture those in their care can become smothering, overprotective and confining.

▶ Love of tradition can turn self-destructive when personal insecurity causes them to be vulnerable to ultra-conservative or ultra-liberal standards or causes.

▶ Being overly compliant or overly rebellious can polarize relationships into friend/foe or for/against constellations.

▶ Their desire to respond to others' needs can cause them to become scattered and feel overburdened and resentful.

▶ Inclinations to become over-directive or under-directive increase rigidity and inflexibility, leaving little room for others to be creative and take initiative.

Ways to Develop Relationships and Spiritual Vitality

▶ Stretch your parameters: for example, once a week listen to people who have different ideas, points of view, values and/or lifestyles. Avoid criticizing or arguing; rather, search for reasons to appreciate what they have to say.

▶ Recognize and resist accusatory attitudes and opinions in you that create resistance and hostility in others.

▶ Before agreeing to do something, stop and take time to clearly evaluate whether or not it is reasonable in the context of your other responsibilities.

➤ Spend time daily in meditation and journaling. Quieting down and getting to know yourself will put you in touch with your inner teacher and natural wisdom.

➤ Confront your inner directive to do things out of responsibility and find another motive, like love or appreciation, to be the focus of your intent.

➤ Dream for the future and share your dreams with your partner, family and/or friends, then see what happens.

➤ Devote time to an artistic pursuit and you will find another aspect of you that has lain unconscious for years.

➤ Thinking through the consequences of revealing information to people in your life alleviates the pain of embarrassment or anger.

Wound

Betrayal, a wound to the thinking center, caused the most damage to Sixes. They want to trust themselves but can't. They want to trust others but don't. As children, they may have had too much responsibility and discipline or too little guidance. They were overly protected at one time and set free or ignored at another. What or whom could they trust? Should they be this or do that? Nothing was ever clear. They felt safe at one moment and, to survive, needed to rebel the next. Approval and love came from being responsible, and safety came from being so loyal they would always be included in their primary group. Not being accepted for themselves, everything felt ambiguous; they couldn't find a solid ground on which to stand.

Thus, personal security, plans, decisions, direction, boundaries and confidence in oneself were up for grabs (repressed thinking). Compensating for that dis-ease, they came to depend on their abilities to ask questions and gain information (preferred thinking), to be responsible in their actions (doing) and connect with others (feeling). The strengths they develop both protect and perpetuate their original wound of betrayal as they continue to distrust themselves and others.

Healing this wound begins when Sixes stop their whirling minds, take stock of the relationships they are in, and learn to trust in the people in their lives. One Six we know was physically dependent on her husband for two years due to illness; it was only then that she stated, "I never knew he loved me this much." Resting in the confidence of primary relationships, Sixes can then evaluate and let go of the apprehension they feel about life in general. Finally, by centering in themselves, they can face the central question that betrayal creates, "Am I essentially flawed?" and answer it from their soul with a profound, "No!"

Repressed Virtue

Faith, hope and love are the three virtues needed to become fully human and open to life; the repressed virtue in Sixes is faith.

Faith is trust and courage, and its opposite is fear. Sixes

attempt to compensate for the trust and courage not easily accessible to them by being responsible. They look outside themselves for reassurance and a place to belong. Activity and continual interaction protect them from experiencing the fear that smolders beneath the surface. They replace the virtue of faith with "little beliefs" by which they live their lives. They seek advice and information from many people yet remain uncertain, mistrusting whether it is right. Knowing what others expect from them and having rules to guide them give them some measure of security.

When Sixes finally make the decision to slow down the pace of life, set limits on the time they will spend working and socializing, and set regular times for prayer and reflection, they become attuned to the Inner Teacher. Guided by Spirit, they enter the Source of light where their souls are renewed with the joy of courageous trust.

Forgotten Child

The bright, curious, questioning child was silenced and forgotten as Sixes slowly became convinced that so-called "truth" was as changeable as the weather. Because they couldn't trust the information they received, the secure, joyful aspects of their soul — once so alive and open — were silenced as responsibility and adaptability helped them feel safe and loved in the world.

Sixes reclaim the energy of this vital part of themselves every time they look within for the wisdom they need. Taking the risk to trust themselves, being open to new ideas and ways of doing things, suspending judgments about people who live by different values, and forgiving people who don't deserve it, including themselves, allow the vitality of the child to bring balance and harmony into their lives.

Orientation to Time

Sixes are suspended in the "now" and therefore are tyrannized by the immediate. You don't need faith or trust or even courage to deal with the immediate. Thus, Sixes focus on their daily responsibilities to their family, community, professional group or other primary reference group. Upon waking each day, they know fairly well what they are going to do and what is expected of them. They've learned to cope with tension by finding a safe group to which they can belong. They ensure their continued inclusion by working hard and being responsible. As Sixes develop their repressed thinking center, they are released from the tyranny of the immediate and relax into the peace of the present moment.

Challenge

The most important quest for Sixes is to discover the still point within, that inner place in which they can rest from their constant activity and let go of the anxiety that underlies it. They are propelled into responsible action by their energetic doing center; they relate with others with their alert feeling center. Information and decisions are important to them (preferred thinking) while they don't know how much is enough information or how to make decisions (repressed thinking). They question themselves, and this is the origin of their constant low-grade apprehension in daily life.

Therefore, Sixes need to be still, contemplate and focus on a specific issue or problem, trusting that intuition and insight will arise from their soul. Only in silence do they learn to trust their own impressions and their thinking processes; when they try to accomplish this goal in dialogue with another person, they subtly and unconsciously value the other person's perception over their own. Expressing themselves artistically reinforces their trust in their inner selves. As they persist in manifesting their creative impulses, Sixes incarnate their unique vision of the world and the meaning they find in it.

Summary of Type Six

Avoidance. Apprehension.

Passion. Fear.

Preferred center. Thinking.

Dominant center. Feeling or Doing.

Support center. Doing or Feeling.

Repressed center. Thinking.

Stance. Dependent.

Orientation to time. Immediate.

Wound. Betrayal.

Repressed virtue. Faith.

Forgotten child. Bright, curious, questioning child.
Divine image. Endurance or Prophetic Vision.

Questions for Reflection for Sixes

1. Gandhi said, "Forgiveness is the virtue of the brave." What do I gain and/or lose by refusing to forgive past transgressions?

2. When my opinions and judgments cause conflict with others, how specifically could I attempt to see the issue from their point of view?

3. What are the specific reasons I resist or fear the meditation and reflection that would give me the guidance I need?

4. Instead of complaining when situations and/or relationships start to turn negative, what are three constructive steps I could take to improve the situation?

5. What are the particular ways I create the situations that lead to my feeling resentful and overburdened, and how could I prevent this from happening?

6. Who are the people I most admire and most dislike? What positive and negative qualities do they possess, and what keeps me from seeing similar strengths and weaknesses in myself?

7. What ten positive qualities would a bright, curious, questioning child possess that, if I developed them, would help me find balance and harmony within?

SEVEN: THE DREAMER

Quick Overview

Thumbnail sketch. Sevens are optimistic, happy and fun-loving idealists who can't admit there are problems that can't be solved or situations that can't be fixed. These are often mentally creative people with overactive minds, but who also have difficulty following through on their plans and ideas without the support of more practical people. Socially charming, Sevens are enthusiastic communicators who inspire and motivate others.

Humor comes naturally to them and they enjoy entertaining others. They express love for others through loyalty and thoughtfulness while avoiding any direct communication of intimate emotion. Sevens feel caught in the pain of life and strive to avoid it; they want to feel happy.

Positive descriptors. Stimulating, cheerful, lively, entertaining, delightful, appreciative, youthful, optimistic, humorous, entrepreneurial, creative visionaries, skilled conversationalists.

Negative descriptors. Self-indulgent, insensitive, sarcastic, shallow, unrealistic, impulsive, irresponsible, procrastinating, stubborn, overly optimistic, fantasizers, escapists.

Checklist

If you are a Seven, it's likely that you:

☐ Are known for your enthusiasm, sunny disposition and

humor.

- [ ] Are a sociable person who always has something to talk about and knows how to keep the conversation going.
- [ ] Line up several fun activities for your time off and often decide only at the last minute which ones you'll do.
- [ ] Like most people and enjoy helping them whenever you can.
- [ ] Experience other people's expectations as limiting your freedom and tend to resent and reject them.
- [ ] Feel that life's challenges are opportunities to pull out all the stops and prove you're clever enough to beat them.
- [ ] Have an inventive mind, but your love of new experiences can distract you from following through on your ideas.
- [ ] Like to work in team situations in which everyone's enthusiasm about a project keeps the ball rolling and everyone's strengths can make up for each person's weaknesses.
- [ ] Respond to intense situations by finding a humorous side to them, changing the topic, or leaving the situation physically or mentally.
- [ ] Find it easy to come up with solutions to world situations or other people's problems.
- [ ] Are stimulated by intellectual sparring and being on the cutting edge of a new venture.
- [ ] Are "turned off" at the thought of your life being stable, secure and routine.

What's Going On Inside

Center configuration. Sevens see and *interpret* the world through the thinking center, which focuses their interest on information, logic and discovering patterns. They *make sense* of life with the thinking and doing intelligences, which orient them to their own actions and to experience. Repressed feeling causes them to dismiss the importance of emotions in themselves and in others, and to deal with relationships superficially. They mechanically respond to life by protecting

Doing Supports Thinking

Spontaneous and enthusiastic
Fun-loving, playful and entertaining
Do whatever will make their life easier

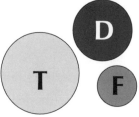

Thinking Is Preferred

Plans to improve their
   world
Active minds
Endless ideas
Multiple interests
Thoughtful
Humorous

Feeling Is Repressed

Express emotion indirectly
Express love as loyalty
Can ignore the emotional
   content in a relationship
Socially charming
Communicators

their freedom; they evaluate their opportunities and choose to do what gratifies them.

Preferred center and dominant center. Thinking is the preferred/dominant center of intelligence in Sevens. They are forward-thinking people who easily conceptualize and initiate new plans, projects and possibilities. Problems or obstacles are simply opportunities that challenge them to send their creative thought processes into high gear, confident that a solution can always be found. Sevens are usually multi-talented with a broad range of interests and knowledge about many topics from science to trivia to philosophy. Sevens tend to be known for their humor (which finds its origin in the thinking center). They're often known as the life of the party and the person who will brighten your day. For Sevens, keeping a positive attitude and dreaming new dreams seems as vital to life as breathing.

Support center. The doing intelligence supports thinking in Sevens. Their active, energetic and spontaneous style makes it nearly impossible to stay with anything routine for very long. They need variety to keep them interested, stay open to new possibilities, and maintain their freedom. As one Seven told us, "I always keep lots of balls in the air. That way if you lose one, who cares?" Endowed with an easy outgoing charm, they have spent a lifetime interacting and staying in contact with people from all walks of life. When they want something, they can be insistent without appearing overbearing—more like a velvet covered jackhammer.

Repressed center. Sevens are often surprised when they discover they repress the feeling intelligence. Because they like to make people happy and people enjoy their company, Sevens can delude themselves into thinking they have a rich emotional life. However, what they most often have is a rich social life guided by good intentions and idealism. Commitment is not their strong suit. Sevens thrive on challenges but feel imprisoned by expectations. When the newness wears off of the relationship they begin to see the imperfections and feel weighed down by the burden of the other person's expectations. Although they prefer loose attachments, once they establish a bond with someone, little if anything can break it.

The First Steps in Soul Development

The team of the thinking center (curiosity) supported by doing (activity) in the Seven creates the illusion that life is about experiencing whatever makes them feel happy. The way the centers interact with each other in Sevens creates the compulsion to live for and feel entitled to as much pleasure as they can experience.

Transformation for Sevens begins in separating the thinking center from the doing center so each can achieve its true purpose. Primarily, all that Sevens know about the doing center is what the thinking center calls from it to support its agenda of curiosity and entitlement. Generally, what is missing from the doing center is purposefulness, drive, the power to accomplish personal goals, and the desire to put forth any effort to contribute something to the lives of other people. When Sevens begin to develop these gifts and use them consciously and unselfishly, their lives take on a new richness and meaning. With this awareness, they also access the creativity of the thinking center to elevate their minds. They learn to ponder life and decide what kind of integrity, value and quality they want their lives to reflect.

The next step in personal transformation for Sevens is to value the true purpose of the feeling center. Sevens often have deep feeling for others but rarely share it directly, choosing instead to express it, for example, by staying connected by phone and e-mail or by doing thoughtful things for those they love. By directly expressing their emotion they reap the harvest of fulfillment in relationship and also begin to see people's dignity and worth as human beings. As their freedom to connect emotionally with the universe and the divine grows, they discover the spiritual principles they need to guide them with meaning and purpose.

Expression of balance. When Sevens explore the path of transformation, they express the quality of fortitude.

Formula for the Passion of Gluttony

Preferred thinking in Sevens creates a mind that can imagine and plan endlessly. The doing center supports thinking first by focusing the plans on experiences and then providing the energy and enthusiasm to accomplish the plans. Repressed feeling means that other people's agendas matter little. The only result that's possible from these forces inter-acting is self-indulgence or gluttony. Sevens' excessiveness could be in areas as diverse as sports, travel, work or sex. Their lives overflow with endless experiences that delight themselves and others.

Core Strengths

► Leadership through brilliant ideas and plans enthusiastically communicated inspire their team to follow through.

► Challenges release their creativity to not only measure up to but to go beyond — ". . . to where no one has gone before."

► Their optimistic energy along with their positive, open and easy response to people creates an atmosphere that dispels most negativity before it can have destructive results.

► They welcome other peoples' ideas, affirm them and invite them to participate in meetings, projects and activities.

► They are acquainted with a wide variety of people and excel at connecting those with common interests or people who could further each other's careers.

► Often considered visionaries, they are intuitively aware of potential possibilities to be taken advantage of before anyone else; they are also aware of potential pitfalls to avoid.

Potential Obstacles

▶ The tendency to rationalize and justify themselves prevents Sevens from looking clearly at situations and relationships that need to be dealt with.

▶ By avoiding the fortitude and hard work required to actualize their dreams, they can lose their energy and love of life.

▶ Their unwillingness to say yes to a relationship, an invitation or a consistent responsibility leads to hurt, resentment and finally an alienation even by those who love them most.

▶ Being entertainers and story tellers in addition to avoiding the commitments of real life can lead to living out their fantasies rather than living their lives.

▶ Their tendency to jump from one project to another, one person to another, one job to another, one experience to another can eventually lead to disillusionment and loneliness.

▶ Looking at life through rose-colored glasses will never produce the freedom of experiencing the true joy and wonder of life.

Ways to Develop Relationships and Spiritual Vitality

▶ Talk half as much and learn to listen without interrupting.

▶ Set aside time every week for inspirational or spiritual reading.

▶ Practice meditation daily.

▶ Start a personal journal that focuses on your feelings and relationships. Begin with a list of feeling words, consulting a thesaurus or dictionary if necessary.

▶ Practice direct non-defensive communication when you have problems or difficult issues to deal with. Changing the topic or saying little hoping the storm will blow over undermines the relationship and doesn't resolve anything.

▶ If you want to grow relationally and spiritually, start facing the painful issues of your life head on.

▶ Examine your relationships to see where you are avoiding commitment either with mental rationalizations or by physically escaping them, and adjust your course in those relationships accordingly.

▶ Ask someone you trust to periodically review your progress and give you a reality check.

Wound

The original wound of Sevens, emotional isolation, inflicted the deepest injury to the feeling center, which then was repressed. Often they grew up in a home in which emotions were repressed and/or emotional turmoil among other family members remained unresolved. With little emotional nurturing, they learned to nurture themselves and retreat into their own fantasies. As children, they quickly realized always being upbeat and entertaining produced the greatest rewards. Sevens learned to survive through bright conversation, laughter, and keeping life light and interesting.

As Sevens created a surreal world of idealism and fantasy, they became disconnected from the practical realities of life and relationships. When pain or adversity came into their lives, they would simply reframe it, often through humor, into a happy or funny episode they could use to entertain others. The mental world where nothing is impossible became the pain-free zone where they lived their real life.

Healing the wound of emotional isolation begins when Sevens develop and strengthen their repressed feeling intelligence. The following suggestions could initiate the healing process: Make the conscious choice to develop fortitude by dealing directly with uncomfortable or painful situations as they arise. Avoid making excuses like, "I've learned the lesson I was meant to learn; now it's time to move on" once the initial rosy glow of a new relationship fades. Journaling, meditation and talking directly and honestly about your feelings help reconnect with life and with the true self.

Repressed Virtue

As they learned that only their bright, cheerful, entertaining qualities were acceptable to others, Sevens experienced emotional isolation and lost contact with the virtue of love. Out of the fear of being rejected, they learned not to trust anyone with the secrets of their heart.

Sevens' greatest treasure was hidden safely away, first from others and then from themselves. Love became a distasteful word laced with the endless demands and expectations from others that would curtail their freedom. With charm and flight they protected themselves from becoming "prisoners" of love as they understood it.

When Sevens can muster the courage to risk revealing the treasures of their heart to others, the virtue of love begins to glow. The illusion of freedom, which they spent so much energy trying to protect, becomes an authentic soul freedom greater than they had ever imagined. Love awakened becomes a spiritual energy flowing from the majestic Source through their soul into the world.

Forgotten Child

The gentle, loving, spiritual child was forgotten as Sevens learned it was unacceptable to express their feelings. Only the nice, happy feelings were permitted; anything else resulted in ridicule and/or rejection. As the disarmingly vulnerable and loving aspects of their true self receded, the sparkling inquisitiveness of thinking and the energetic activity of doing came forward to compensate for the loss.

Sevens recover the treasures embodied in this mystical child each time they stay with, rather than flee from, shared intimacy and feelings of vulnerability. Each time they stay present and listen to someone in difficulty (rather than immediately trying to solve the problem with logical advice or money) they access the loving, gentle child within. Each time they enter into the stillness of their own hearts and listen to the whisper of the divine within, they come to know more deeply what it means to be a spiritual being.

Orientation to Time

Sevens' lives are focused on the future, where they are unfettered by any problems or difficulties in the present. Since they repress the virtue of love and can't love what doesn't yet exist, by living in the future they are free to float on the fresh breeze of possibilities and dreams. However, their feet don't touch the ground long enough to make their dreams a reality. Without breaking this compulsively forward thrust and grounding themselves in the reality of the present moment, they create a future of a life never lived.

Challenge

The most important quest for Sevens is to become conscious of the inner workings of their own souls through appreciating their emotional lives. Sevens' enthusiastic appreciation of experience — the result of the active and outgoing doing center supporting the curious thinking center — rivets their attention on the outer world. The mind investigates and the doing center follows right along into yet another experience. These two centers overwhelm the feeling center, which would reveal their own and others' emotional needs and feelings and alter Sevens' choices. Instead, its sensitive and relational qualities are ignored and pushed aside. All that's left is the never-ending desire for more pleasure.

Sevens enhance their lives when they allow their minds to transcend themselves and enter the universal realm of spirit through balancing head, heart and body. The value of their own emotions eludes them so they miss both the importance of others' emotions and the fulfillment of deep emotional connection with others. As they allow the experience of emotion and relatedness to enter their consciousness, they slow down, become more grounded, and are able to experience the beauty of the present moment because they are living in their souls. They discover they are capable of loving and of commitment, and thus they begin to experience the joy of meaningful, deep relationships.

Summary of Type Seven

Avoidance. Pain.

Passion. Gluttony.

Preferred center. Thinking.

Dominant center. Thinking.

Support center. Doing.

Repressed center. Feeling.

Stance. Aggressive.

Orientation to time. Future.

Wound. Emotional isolation/alienation.

Repressed virtue. Love.

Forgotten child. Gentle, loving, spiritual child.

Divine image. Majesty.

Questions for Reflection for Sevens

1. What is the one essential area of my life that most needs my attention, and what two things could I do to improve that situation?

2. What is the most important dream for my life that I have let slip through my fingers, and what prevents me from accomplishing it now?

3. When I pressure other people to see things from my point of view, what is the egocentric attitude in me that I need to deal with?

4. What commitment do I most resist making, and what specific fears underlie that resistance?

5. What in other people triggers my anger and/or impatience, and how is that same characteristic present in me?

6. My resistance to inner work indicates there is something in me I fear facing. What is it?

7. What are ten strengths a loving, spiritual, gentle child possesses that would enhance my life if I developed them?

EIGHT: THE CONFRONTER

Quick Overview

Thumbnail sketch. Eights come across as forthright, blunt, firm, and full of life and strength. Some are loud and raucous, others are reserved and proper, but all are direct in communication. They have clearly defined ideas on what is just and use their considerable strength to make the world conform to their ideas, first for themselves and then for others. Eights are organized people who are natural leaders.

A hidden tender side often causes them to be protective of their family, children, and anyone whom they consider to be unprotected or oppressed. Secretly, they often feel that life and other people are moving too slowly, and it's their job to make life more interesting. Eights feel caught in their personal weakness and so strive to avoid it; they want to feel strong.

Positive descriptors. Self-reliant, self-assured, strong, truthful, passionate, realistic, direct, assertive, protective, visionary, clear communicators, selfless lovers.

Negative descriptors. Intimidating, insensitive, bossy, excessive, overbearing, abrasive, stubborn, literal, blunt, cold, tough, arrogant.

Checklist

If you're an Eight, it's likely that you:

☐ Enjoy having influence in all situations important to you, either from behind the scenes or in obvious leadership.

☐ Find it natural to manage resources and expect that at least your fair share of this world's good fortune will come your way.

☐ Attempt to make your presence strongly felt in the physical world because inside you can feel unimportant.

☐ Can feel almost invisible until there's a crisis and people need your strength and competency.

☐ Can fight for a cause you know is right and let the chips fall where they may.

☐ Can be gentle, warm and affectionate when you are around children, with animals, or in service to those who are oppressed.

☐ Can use your power to protect and guide your family and are capable of dealing strongly with and even intimidating family members, whether you want to or not.

☐ Are dedicated to values you perceive as important for survival or happiness for family members and friends.

☐ Have clear and firm ideas about what is right and wrong in situations important to you.

☐ Are generally on the alert for people with hidden agendas.

☐ Find that people who never directly say what is on their minds are the most irritating and difficult people to deal with.

☐ Are a practical person who understands what it takes to get the job done.

What's Going On Inside

Center configuration. Because Eights see and *interpret* the world through the doing center, their interest is focused on action, determination and protecting themselves. They *process* information with the thinking and doing intelligences, which orients them to their own actions. Repressed feeling causes them to dismiss the importance of emotions and relationships. Therefore, they mechanically respond to life by purposefully doing all things important to them.

Preferred center and dominant center. Eights draw upon

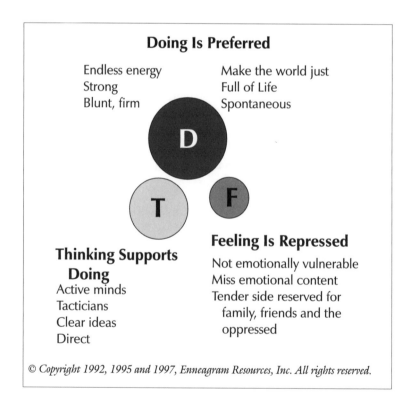

Doing Is Preferred

Endless energy   Make the world just
Strong   Full of Life
Blunt, firm   Spontaneous

D

T   **F**

Thinking Supports Doing
Active minds
Tacticians
Clear ideas
Direct

Feeling Is Repressed
Not emotionally vulnerable
Miss emotional content
Tender side reserved for
    family, friends and the
    oppressed

the vitality of their preferred/dominant doing center for their limitless energy and stamina. They have a lust for life and go after it with extravagance and excess. Because the issues of maintaining personal power and control are vital to them, Eights are always vigilant, determining who is for them and who is against them. They want to keep their support systems solid. They have a bottom-line and often tactless style of communication — direct, blunt, barking orders — highlighted by an abrupt "Don't waste my time" attitude. Their concern for justice leads Eights to be relentless advocates for weak or defenseless people whom they have decided are being treated wrongly. They are at home in the material world, know how to organize and push a project through to completion, and bring zest and excitement into life.

Support center. The logic, cleverness and decisiveness of their support thinking center enhance the determination and cunning of the doing center, making Eights formidable tacticians. They have the ability to think on their feet and process information quickly, so they rarely question the truth of their ideas, perceptions, decisions, actions or prejudices. They are suspicious of information being held from them and of hidden agendas. They themselves are up-front people who want all the issues out on the table so they can be dealt with. Every move that Eights make is calculated and well thought out. These are not risk takers who would take a chance of losing their power, position or money. They have learned to trust their own instincts and abilities to analyze reality.

Repressed center. With their feeling intelligence repressed, Eights use expressiveness, intensity, love of pleasure, and discussing common interests to masquerade as emotional relationship. They connect with others through activity and ideas — doing and thinking — not by sharing feelings. Eights are not aware of or concerned about their own feelings and are not sensitive to (or even tolerant of) people who continually want to talk about how they feel. To them, an emotional approach to life is weak. Eights are attracted to friendships that are independent and free from emotional strings. As one Eight described it, "Real friends are undemanding. They make you feel like you've put on a sweat suit and a comfortable pair of old slippers at the end of a long day. Then they serve you champagne and caviar!"

First Steps in Soul Development

The way the centers of intelligence interact with each other in Eights creates the compulsion to dominate, gain power, stimulate, and energize life to make it move faster so it isn't boring to them.

Reclaiming full personhood for Eights begins in separating the doing and thinking centers so each can attain its true purpose. All that Eights know of the thinking center are its qualities that support the agenda of the doing center — maintaining power and influence and protecting one's safety. When the thinking center is used independently, Eights discover it can also ponder the meaning of situations and of life itself, love to learn for its own sake, and investigate the inner workings of their own soul and psyche. They also learn to use the doing center to gain guidance, be genuine, rest, and experience delight in the present moment.

Another step in personal transformation propels them into the mysteries of the feeling center. Many Eights find it easy to be generous, tender and kind with those who do not threaten their power or safety — children or animals, for example. As they explore ways of using this secret side of themselves with adults and learn how to be emotionally vulnerable, they discover the wonder of emotional connectedness and the joy of reciprocal relationships. Entering their own inner world of feeling opens them to relating to the universe and the divine. Softened, they let down their guard and discover their own value as a human being is intrinsic and not dependent on their use of strength, as they were convinced when they were responding to life automatically.

Expression of balance. As Eights explore the path of transformation, they become compassionate.

Formula for the Passion of Lust

Eights' preferred doing intelligence accesses energy and focuses their interest on their own actions. The thinking center supports doing by justifying any action they want to take. With the feeling center repressed, they dismiss the value of other people's agendas, needs and feelings. It's not that they

151

elicit other people's responses and then dismiss the importance of what they say or feel. Rather, it simply never occurs to them to consult with anyone.

This combination of energies is the formula for lust, a limitless drive toward life and experience — a lust for power, for whatever makes life exciting. They want to be where the action is and do everything that makes them feel alive.

Core Strengths

► Eights' leadership style is marked by vision, hard work, organization and communication that affirms, energizes and encourages people toward dedication and achievement.

► They stand up for others and don't count the cost when dedicated to a person or a cause.

► Their grounded strength and their ability to instantaneously analyze a situation make them masters at dealing with crisis.

► Their stamina, perseverance and ability to handle pressure and stress enable them to complete, close to target date, whatever they begin despite the obstacles or setbacks they have to deal with.

► They encourage others to assert themselves, develop their strengths, and then support and cheer them on in their success.

► Their generosity and influence are often used for the betterment of the community.

Potential Obstacles

► Over-identifying with influence and power can tempt Eights to manipulate and control others.

► Arrogantly convinced that they have the strength to handle anything life tosses their way and too proud to ask for help, they can overextend themselves to the point they are blind sided with burnout.

► They can pay a high price in lost relationships for remaining ignorant of how their overbearing behavior affects others.

► When they use their power in self-serving ways, they leave a wide path of destruction that they and others will have to deal with for years.

► They can convince themselves their subjective ideas about justice are really objective truth and feel self-righteously justified in intimidating and condemning other people with them.

► Ignorant of the impact that their direct, advice-giving style of communication has on others leaves Eights with the illusion of having wonderful open conversations. More often than not, other parties describe these interactions as self-serving, superior monologues that leave them feeling alienated.

Ways to Develop Relationships and Spiritual Vitality

► In relationships, if you are totally convinced you are right, know you are wrong.

153

- ► Learn to let go of control and trust that others' ways of doing something may be different from yours but are still effective.
- ► By moderating your overly blunt, intimidating style, you will avoid alienating the very people who most support you.
- ► Allow people to take care of you without indicating how they could do it better the next time.
- ► Practice being grateful for what is, rather than being impatient with what is not yet complete.
- ► Slow down; learn the art of delegating and resting.
- ► Practice meditation daily.
- ► Relax and ask your partner to plan a vacation.

Wound

The core wound in Eights, emotional isolation/alienation, caused the greatest damage to the feeling center intelligence. As children, they often grew up fast and learned to take care of themselves pretty well, as long as their feelings didn't get in the way. Like the daddy three-horned dinosaur sings in *Land Before Time III*, "When life gets tough, ya gotta get tougher. When life gets rough, ya gotta get rougher. It's the only way to survive." Eights learned meeting life head on worked best for them.

Their strength and confidence is apparent to everyone early on. In their youth, older children and even adults often looked to them to handle difficulties. Using their power to take care of themselves and others became a way of life that didn't leave room for display of weakness. Few people know that Eights rarely feel on the inside as strong as they look on the outside.

The difficulty of being strong was that others never saw or allowed them to have needs. As one Eight said, "I felt invisible. No one ever saw *me* unless there was a crisis." Thus, power, influence, keen instincts and cleverness became the values around which they built their lives. Eights, though insensitive to emotional issues, became very aware of justice issues and continue to do what they've done since childhood — take care of those who need their strength.

Healing the wound happens as Eights open and develop their feeling center. Reducing the time and energy they pour into the material world and slowing down the pace of life are important steps toward opening the heart. Prayer, meditation and artistic expression help get in touch with the emotions set aside in childhood. As Eights explore the inner life, they learn to express the strength of soul inherent in compassion.

Repressed Virtue

Of the three great virtues needed for healing and wholeness — faith, hope and love — Eights lost contact with love. They are unable to love themselves because their experience has given them reason to expect people will be insensitive to them. Eights compensate for the loss of love by focusing on their power to control the external world. With their emotions and love repressed, they are free to overuse the doing and thinking centers of intelligence.

When love is repressed, it doesn't mean it isn't there. Rather, it means the fullness of love that would enrich their lives and bring it into harmony is not available to them. Throughout their lives, Eights have learned to express the love they feel for others by protecting them so they feel safe and secure. When Eights surrender their power to the Source of power, their soul is energized. Their goal is now learning how to conquer with love, with their hearts being their only weapon or defense.

Forgotten Child

The spiritual, loving, gentle child was left behind and forgotten in the garden of childhood as Eights' emotional needs were minimized and unfulfilled. Without the confidence of tender belonging that would have developed had these childlike aspects been nurtured, Eights had to carve out their own place of belonging in the world. Thus, the power and energy of the doing center and the clever analysis of the thinking center came forward to help them make the world their home.

Eights awaken and embrace the child in the garden through prayer, reflection, meditation, sharing their feelings with other people, and artistic creation. When they let their fists of power relax into open hands, they are ready to receive the fullness of the lost mystical child.

Orientation to Time

Having lost the virtue of love, Eights are free to focus on the future because they can't and don't need to love what does not yet exist. Eights are determined to go after life with gusto. They move forward so quickly, they leave most everyone else in the dust. If they don't bring this compulsive pattern to a halt, they miss the love and beauty that can only be found in the present moment, and they set up a barren future. By slowing down the pace of life, they can appreciate where they are, whom they are with, and what they are doing.

Challenge

The most important quest for Eights is to awaken the visionary within and access the spiritual values that provide a counterbalance to their extraordinary ability to manage the assets of the physical world. By dismissing the transcendent and relational values of their repressed feeling center, Eights feel justified in using their tremendous power and strength to dominate people and/or control situations. The doing center provides the energy and purposefulness, and the thinking center provides the plan. This is the origin of their dynamism and their ability to maneuver themselves into power positions.

Eights need to develop their spiritual side; prayer and/or meditation are important ways to slow down and understand life from a point of view that is less obvious when they're in the thick of things. As they develop both emotionally and mentally, they discover the conscious and creative use of imagination supports their growth by expanding their horizons and deepening their expression of emotion. By turning inward, they also discover the soul dimensions they thought were missing; then they are able to share themselves in relationships with kindness and tenderness as well as with strength.

As they experience a fuller breadth of their own personhood and their own innate goodness, they come to value themselves in ways they demanded others value them when they were responding to life automatically.

Summary of Type Eight
Avoidance. Weakness.
Passion. Lust.
Preferred center. Doing.
Dominant center. Doing.
Support center. Thinking.
Repressed center. Feeling.
Stance. Aggressive.
Orientation to time. Future.
Wound. Emotional isolation/alienation.
Repressed virtue. Love.
Forgotten child. Gentle, loving, spiritual child.
Divine image. Foundation.

Questions for Reflection for Eights
1. How specifically do I impose my ideas of justice on other

people, and how is my ego being served when I do this?

2. In what specific areas would my learning to be more adaptable better serve me and those around me?

3. What five positive things could happen if I loosened or let go of control in each of the following areas: work, family, community?

4. What fear am I avoiding when I continue to resist slowing down, meditation and reflection?

5. How might everyone benefit if I re-examine my attitudes that cause tension in my closest relationships?

6. What attitudes or characteristics in other people anger me? How are variations of these same qualities present in me?

7. What ten positive qualities would a spiritual, loving, gentle child possess that would benefit me and those I love if I developed them?

NINE: THE PRESERVATIONIST

Quick Overview

Thumbnail sketch. Nines are easygoing, affable people who are professionally and socially respected. They recoil from conflict of any kind and withdraw into the passive power of silence to ward off what they experience as emotional upheaval. Professionally, these unflappable people prove to be practical, deliberate and resourceful. They have the resilience to deal with situations others find too stressful.

Because Nines expend nearly all of their energy in the public and social forums, their private world tends to be neglected emotionally, physically and spiritually. They use agreeability and friendliness to get along with others. When pressed into situations they don't want to be in, they often retaliate passive-aggressively. Nines feel caught in turmoil and strive to avoid it; they want to feel peaceful.

Positive descriptors. Affable, resourceful, tolerant, gentle, kind, patient, unflappable, unassuming, diplomatic, unpretentious, harmonious, non-judgmental.

Negative descriptors. Secretive, indirect, unforgiving, noncommittal, unfocused, lethargic, indifferent, neglectful, complacent, resistant, passive-aggressive, self-forgetful.

Checklist

If you're a Nine, it's likely that you:

☐ Are known for being friendly and affable even when inside

you feel very different.

☐ Generally like to get along with others, even to the point of verbally agreeing with them and then privately doing what you want or intended all along.

☐ Reserve personal communication to very few people.

☐ Are willing to do your work but also conserve a good portion of your time for relaxation and play.

☐ Don't like to fight, argue or push yourself to get ahead.

☐ Generally hold your competitive drive in check and expend it in games and sports.

☐ Prefer living by routines you can rely on and find changes in schedules or plans distasteful and/or annoying.

☐ Have a place in your home to which you gravitate when nothing else is going on.

☐ Find yourself resolving conflicts and/or dealing with failure by saying things like "It doesn't matter" or "It's no big deal."

☐ Can find yourself dwelling on past offenses and feeling caught in unresolved emotions, which cause you to believe others don't value you as much as they do other people.

☐ Feel best about yourself when you have a good reputation and know you've earned the respect of others.

☐ Enjoy outdoor activities and find in nature a source of freedom and peace.

What's Going On Inside

Center configuration. Nines see and *interpret* the world through the doing center but then don't use that center when they are trying to make sense of the information they have received. Preferred doing focuses their interest on activity, determination and protecting themselves. At the level of *processing* information, they make sense out of life with the thinking and feeling intelligences, which means they internalize information, overvalue their own interpretation of it, but then dismiss the value of acting on the information. Thus, not acting responsibly becomes more important than acting,

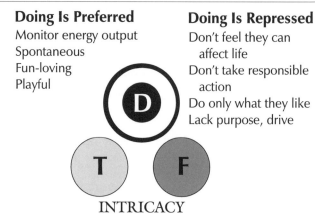

Doing Is Preferred
Monitor energy output
Spontaneous
Fun-loving
Playful

Doing Is Repressed
Don't feel they can
    affect life
Don't take responsible
    action
Do only what they like
Lack purpose, drive

INTRICACY

Thinking Supports Feeling
Love puzzles and mysteries
Technically proficient
Clever and insightful
Problem solvers for others

Feeling Supports Thinking
Affable
Get along well with others
Don't want to offend others
Don't like emotionally
    charged situations

determination turns into stubbornness, and protecting their own safety becomes preeminent. They mechanically respond to life by protecting their safety and keeping their thoughts and feelings to themselves while pondering them.

Preferred center. The ability of Nines to make their way in the world comes from using only the shell of the doing intelligence. Preferred doing makes Nines hyper-aware of their energy output. They devote the major portion of their energy to their work life. Yet, when work is over, they feel their free time is their own. Nines are often playful people who enjoy spontaneous activity, thereby making life interesting and fun. They are experts at not taking life too seriously and often have a well developed repertoire of favorite recreational activities.

Many Nines are attracted to outdoor activities, since nature holds the peace and beauty that soothes the gnawing sense of pressure created by life's responsibilities. As long as Nines can be in an unpressured environment free from unexpected demands, they have great stamina for working at a steady pace for long hours. When outside pressure builds, Nines become tense, feeling almost paralyzed and unable to effect the situation.

Support centers and dominant center. Nines use the thinking and feeling centers to make sense out of life, which makes them competent in complicated situations, a strength they use primarily in the workplace, not at home. Often devising enlightened solutions to problems in the outer world, they especially appreciate recognition on the job because they generally think so little of themselves.

Their access to the feeling center is obvious in the way they get along with most people and are usually likable, affable and friendly. They dislike contention of any kind to the point that when someone disagrees with them or confronts them, they easily switch their positions verbally and later do what they want. Their style of relating is to merge with the other person. They can live vicariously through their partner or children, believing the other person's achievements are in some way their own as well. In this way, Nines don't stand out and don't want to stand out.

Because no two things in nature can grow exactly equally, either the thinking or the feeling intelligence dominates in any particular Nine. The other center then supports the first as the Nine processes the impressions he or she receives from life.

Repressed Center. With the doing center out of the picture when it comes to making sense out of life, Nines tend to be slow and steady people whose view of what needs to be done is often fuzzy. They easily become distracted from their goal. As one Nine told us, "The style of the Nine is to start slow . . . and then taper off." They can be passive-aggressive in relationships, a quality that easily sabotages their alliances, friendships, and even their intimate relationships in the family. Most Nines have a place in the home where they can usually be found when nothing else is going on.

First Steps in Soul Development

The team of the thinking center (cleverness and analysis) and feeling center (affability and gentleness) feed information to each other. Nines present themselves to the world through the surface values of the doing center (pleasurable activity and safety). This creates the illusion that Nines need to be protected from the pressures of life and have the right to experience the peace they seek. Because the doing center is repressed, its native assertiveness, strength and drive — which would create the self-confidence and the self-esteem that Nines need — are unavailable. The way the centers interact in Nines creates the compulsion to be indirect and passive-aggressive when dealing with life's pressures and to be affable but nonpersonal in dealing with people.

Discovering true personhood for type Nine begins in separating the thinking and feeling centers so each can achieve its true purpose. Nines who choose transformation discover the thinking center's capacity for creative thought, discovery, the ability to investigate one's own psyche, and the ability to ponder life until its meaning becomes clear. Similarly, they unlock the feeling center's capacity to synthesize many aspects of reality into a new understanding. Artistic creativity, a passion for life, and emotional connectedness to other people are other results.

Another step in personal transformation for type Nine is to discover the true purpose of the doing center. Releasing the doing center means discovering its ability to lend intent, purposefulness and drive on the one hand, and guidance, genuineness and joy of life on the other. The result is a person who is in touch with his or her innate goodness and who is willing to share from a vast storehouse of giftedness to make a contribution to life and to people.

Expression of balance. As Nines explore their potential for transformation, they become diligent in pursuit of their life goals.

The Formula for the Passion of Sloth

Preferred doing makes action a value. Repressed doing makes action seem frivolous, useless, or close to impossible. The outcome of this inner conflict can only be paralysis expressed as sloth or laziness.

This situation is reinforced by the thinking and feeling centers playing off each other. Nines have feelings about their ideas and analyze their feelings, but no course of action ever comes of this internal processing. Inside Nines, it's like they have one foot on the gas and the other on the brake: high powered stop. The engine whirrs but the car doesn't go anywhere.

Core Strengths

► Nines' leadership style is one of stability, clearly defined roles, harmony, and delegation to a team of people who each follow through on their responsibilities to achieve a common goal.

▶ They are fair-minded people who can listen to and understand everyone's point of view.

▶ They have a natural aptitude for getting along with a wide variety of people, and their warmth and kindness encourage others to trust them.

▶ Their excellent mediation skills allow them to enter difficult situations and bring harmony and resolution.

▶ They are resourceful and creative people who find common sense solutions to problems in the workplace.

▶ Professionally they are stable, responsible, hard working and highly respected.

Potential Obstacles

▶ Their need to maintain peace often prevents them from taking a stand that needs to be taken until it's too late.

▶ They can become so identified with others that they forget or don't express their own needs.

▶ In their compulsion to take the path of least resistance, they can abandon their integrity and compromise their core values.

▶ Their self-forgetfulness often results in not caring for themselves physically, emotionally, intellectually and/or spiritually.

▶ Their consistent silence about their own needs or desires eventually leads to resentment and taking out anger on others in passive-aggressive ways.

▶ The lack of inner direction results in doing unimportant

things and leaving important things undone.

Ways to Develop Relationships and Spiritual Vitality

➤ Take a stand and, if necessary, change it later. In the words of Anthony de Mello, "People who deliberate fully before they take a step will spend their lives on one leg."

➤ Make a chart: primary areas of interest and responsibility listed on the left side (with an emphasis on personal relationships) and three columns headed "three month goal," " six month goal" and "one year goal." Fill in each box.

➤ Find someone to hold you accountable to your goals; meet regularly to assess how you are progressing.

➤ Clearly identify resentments from your past; one-by-one find healing and resolution for them and let them go.

➤ Take stock of your significant relationships by asking and answering this question: "What are three specific things I could do to let these people know how much I love them and/or how much they mean to me?"

➤ Pursue an intellectual or artistic endeavor that is a secret interest of yours and pursue it with passion.

➤ Notice what needs to be done practically in and around your residence and accomplish these tasks the way they need to be done (no shortcuts!) and without being asked.

➤ Search for the specific areas in which you experience a merged identity with your partner and/or with other significant people in your life, discovering how you can establish your own unique identity in these areas.

Wound

Abandonment is the wound that damaged Nines' doing center. The abandonment could be physical and/or emotional, anything from an absent parent to emotional rejection to a caregiver who was not emotionally available. Whatever the particulars of the situation, Nines felt adrift as children, growing up without guidance. Because of the absence of the love that children innately know should be there for them, they came to believe that they were damaged goods. To protect themselves, they became acutely aware of emotional atmospheres so that, when tension built, they knew how to escape and create a cocoon of safety. They chose activities alone or with others that kept them from feeling and dealing with pressure. As adults, Nines perpetuate this wound by abandoning others and themselves.

Nines find healing by looking straight into a mirror of truth. This first step is the hardest one for them. Once life brings them up short enough to make them look within, they find ample talents and strengths for the inner journey. They often need support from another person in outlining their responsibilities, and in naming and achieving their life goals. In this process, they find the joy of connecting with themselves, others and life.

Repressed Virtue

Of the three virtues needed for healing, Nines find hope least accessible. Into its place slips wishful thinking, which distracts them from developing the strength of soul that is hope. Pinning their dreams on the expectation that outer circumstances should go their way, Nines experience the disappointment that comes from not taking their lives into their own hands.

Nines access the virtue of hope when they use the clarity of their thinking intelligence, not to analyze feelings, but to direct their doing. Similarly, they motivate their doing by using the feeling intelligence, not to understand complicated thoughts, but to be passionate about what they do. Then, the Source of all hope comes to meet them, and they discover the stabilizing and life giving presence called soul.

Forgotten Child

It is the adventuresome, spontaneous, playful child that Nines left on the playground of childhood. At first glance, this may seem odd because Nines protect their time for play, relaxation and enjoying life. However, in compulsion, Nines' playfulness is a way of staving off pressure and responsibility, and of distracting themselves from the hard work of the journey inward. It is not the truly free playfulness inspired by the adventuresome inner child. As children, Nines found these aspects of themselves were either ignored, misunderstood or even disciplined. Therefore, the more inward qualities such as curiosity and gentleness came forward as more boisterous qualities receded.

Nines incorporate the gifts of the adventuresome inner child as they choose the greatest adventure of all — the quest for their own souls. Here they discover the joy available when one truly knows oneself and shares with others from this core experience of one's own humanity.

Orientation to Time

Nines in compulsion focus on the past. They think about the good and bad of their lives, analyzing their experiences but keeping most of their reflections to themselves. They feel incapable of using their positive qualities for anyone's benefit, and they feel powerless to find healing for the pain they have experienced. As long as they cling to the past, failing to resolve its conflicts and letting them go, they will be walking backward into the future. Necessarily, they stumble over life's obstacles. When Nines choose to look directly into the mirror of truth, they find the satisfaction that comes with living in the present moment.

Challenge

The most important quest for Nines is to open the realms of the soul and the unconscious and locate the sacred point that radiates from the center of their being. The feeling of being unimportant (common to the Eight, Nine and One, all of whom prefer the doing center) combines in type Nine with the sense of futility created by simultaneously repressing the doing center, the center of action, accomplishment and joy in living. With this "double dose" of self-negation, so to speak, Nines in compulsion are afraid to look within because they falsely believe they will find nothing there. This is the origin of their inability to affirm themselves and their need to deflect sources of conflict and distress.

As Nines listen to the voice that proceeds from their soul, they discover the true nature of their being is strong, resilient and spiritual. By appreciating their hidden talents, they formulate goals for their lives. They realize life has purpose and they have something to contribute. Nines generally love nature but use it as a peaceful refuge from the pressures of the world. As they accept the challenge to connect with their own souls, Nines experience an uplifting awareness of the sacredness of physical reality.

Summary of Type Nine

Avoidance. Conflict/distress.

Passion. Sloth.

Preferred center. Doing.

Dominant center. Thinking or feeling.

Support center. Feeling or thinking.

Repressed center. Doing.

Stance. Withdrawing.

Orientation to time. Past.

Wound. Abandonment.

Repressed virtue. Hope.

Forgotten child. Adventuresome, spontaneous, playful child.

Divine image. Presence.

Questions for Reflection for Nines

1. What ten ways do I hurt myself and my relationships by not directly stating my needs?

2. In what specific ways do I disregard and undervalue myself? What do I gain and what do I suffer because of this behavior?

3. What specifically do I lose by not taking charge of a situation that would improve my life?

4. What resentments prevent me from moving on? What three positive and creative solutions would help me let go of these resentments?

5. What tasks in my personal life have I been avoiding? If I completed them how would my life and my relationships improve?

6. How do I use silence to gain control? Whom do I use it against most consistently, and what of lasting value do I gain or lose from this behavior?

7. What are the specific things I could decide to do every day that would help me activate my repressed doing intelligence?

Conclusion

We began chapter 1 with a story about an eagle who sadly believed he was a chicken. Because he believed he was a chicken, he thought, felt and acted like one.

Now, at the end of chapter 2, we realize more fully how that story applies to our lives as described by the Enneagram. In daily life, we usually experience a version of ourselves that is far less than our soul potential would indicate. Therefore, after exploring the nine types and identifying our own place in the Enneagram, we are confronted with one important question: "Which do you want to be, a chicken or an eagle?"

The average state of people is to be confined by the limitations of their personality, as described by the Enneagram compulsion, rather than be liberated by the potential of their personhood, the power of their own soul. The Enneagram describes how our chicken habits keep us earthbound. In the process of personal transformation, we learn to spread our wings and soar with the eagles.

CHAPTER 3

SOUL STRENGTH: LIVING IN THE PRESENT MOMENT

"Be the change you want to see."
— Mohandas K. Gandhi

As a child, he was shy and a poor student who stuttered. He also had big ears; the other children taunted him mercilessly. By the end of his early school years, he felt isolated and afraid to talk in public. However, eventually he earned his law degree and became a barrister in South Africa where he earned a good living.

Late one bitter cold night, he was thrown out of the first class railroad car where he had a valid ticket and tossed off the train. Why? Because he was the wrong color. In the midst of that humiliating experience, he made two decisions that would change his life forever.

First, he decided he would never use force to win a cause. Second, he himself would never again yield to force.

That night, Mohandas K. Gandhi accessed the full potential of his soul. His personal journey would change the face of the twentieth century and would make of him the *mahatma*, the "great soul" who became holy by living for and

175

loving others.

Awakening to the Present Moment

Like Gandhi, we discover and connect to our soul's full potential the moment we make the decision to live a life of love and service. Our decisions and choices in the now allow our soul potential to be revealed in the unfolding of life.

The illusion is to believe we will discover our soul potential at some future time. This attitude prevents us from recognizing we have no power to change anything, including ourselves. It creates the illusion, "If I try hard enough, I will achieve my full soul potential."

In reality, when we make the decision to live a life of love and service, we commit our body, mind, heart and soul to God. God's love and power are limitless; in this way, our soul potential becomes limitless.

How does the Enneagram assist us in living a life guided by Spirit rather than driven by circumstance? When we look at the nine types of the Enneagram from the inside out, we discover how we've built a defense structure that has now become our prison. The Enneagram shows how to dismantle the walls of that prison brick by brick so we can regain our freedom.

The View from the Repressed Center

Fascinating insights result from grouping the nine types according to which center they commonly repress. Viewing the types from this perspective, you discover what is missing from each personality type that creates imbalance and limits its point of view.

Specifically, Ones, Twos and Sixes share the "dependent stance," which is the result of repressing the thinking center. The "aggressive stance" of Threes, Sevens and Eights is the consequence of repressing the feeling center. The "withdrawing stance," which is the outcome of repressing the doing center, is common to Fours, Fives and Nines.

With one center repressed in each type, one of three equally important viewpoints — as well as an entire set of gifts and qualities — is absent. On the other hand, the dominant-support center team left in charge of the personality combines their gifts to create some amazing strengths.

This chapter explores the nine types from the perspective of the three stances that are created by these configurations of centers. Further, when one type exhibits a major quality, the other two types that share the same repressed center will exhibit a variation of that quality. Working with this principle, you can discover many new aspects about the types through observation.

The difficulties caused by repressing one center are more obvious in your personal life. Therefore, the repercussions of repressing a center look very different from what you may at first assume.

Professionally, people develop the skills needed to feel confident in the workplace. For example, people with a repressed thinking center can have multiple graduate degrees, people with a repressed feeling center often have myriad relationships and varied artistic talents, and people with a repressed doing center can responsibly manage their jobs with great efficiency. Therefore, what the Enneagram points out by saying we each repress one of our three native intelligences is in an entirely different arena — that of our private lives in which we feel free to "be ourselves."

While this is a practical chapter, it still relates to soul development. Real personal growth must be grounded in our day-to-day lives. Any spiritual advancement that doesn't effect practical change is illusionary and merely massages the ego.

By describing the standard approach that people who repress each of the three centers take in life, then highlighting the strengths and detailing an agenda for growth for each stance, we explore possibilities for soul expansion. This process results in greater fulfillment because we are living more consistently from our souls.

THE DEPENDENT STANCE

Three types have a repressed thinking center, Ones, Twos and Sixes. This doesn't mean they don't or can't think. As a matter of fact, they often experience themselves as thinking too much because, when the thinking center is undeveloped, it thinks nonproductively. Then the thinking process has to be repeated. Issues become connected with each other and can't be sorted out and settled one at a time. These types find it difficult to say no directly, and if they say no, they often don't mean it. They have difficulty placing boundaries in their lives.

Since these types tucked the thinking center away as children because it was wounded, it has not matured along with the rest of the person. This core problem produces many qualities these three types share in common.

Most importantly, their consistent unconscious stance is to look to the situation to see what should happen next. Placing their reference point outside themselves is the core meaning of "dependent." If they dismiss the ability to think for themselves because the thinking center is out of the picture when they're trying to make sense out of life, other people and situations set their agenda.

However, Ones, Twos and Sixes set the standards. Because they have difficulty evaluating themselves, high standards assure them their performance will be acceptable. Consternation arises: they must do well at whatever the situation or people around them expect, want or need.

All of them are tyrannized by the immediate situation: Ones by what needs to be done right now, Twos by the person in front of them who needs their help, and Sixes by their daily responsibilities and schedules. It is difficult for these types to plan ahead because everything depends on what the day and the people in it will ask of them.

All three types tend to be opinionated. Opinions are an example of undeveloped thinking. They are ideas from 20 years ago that have never been reexamined to see if they are still meaningful. Or they are ideas inherited from family or culture and have never been thought through to discover what they mean. (When you think through an opinion for yourself and come to your own conclusion, then the idea becomes a conviction.) If the thinking center is undeveloped, it's easier to assimilate ideas from others and from the culture.

Because the clarity of the thinking center is blocked, these types may need to have information repeated, may interrupt other people with their own observations or questions, and may even interrupt themselves by starting a sentence, not completing it, then starting another sentence. Also, they easily ask questions of others about issues that, if they took a minute to think about, they would realize they already know the answer. Questioning others rather than themselves points to their lack of trust in their own thinking process.

Because the clarity and objectivity that a mature thinking center would bring is unavailable to them, these types are driven by an unconscious apprehension that they disguise, even to themselves, with graciousness and activity. Due to this uneasiness, these types tend to overestimate the cost in money, time and materials when planning a project.

Strengths
► Dependent types tend to be chatty and sociable.
► They are excellent networkers.
► They are known for being gracious and charming.

- In groups, they prefer that everyone get along.
- Their desire is to relate rather than to isolate.
- They tend to champion the basic values of their reference group. The quality of their morals and ideals depends on the group to which they adhere. For example, the value "honor among thieves" could easily have been developed by dependent types within that social subgroup.
- Dependent types tend to be highly dedicated to their profession and/or primary reference group.
- In ordinary society and institutions, they tend to be those pillars upon whom everyone depends to make the organization work, the project happen, the group function as a unit.
- They have great tenacity for the project they are involved in at the present. However, if they become disconnected from it they may have a hard time getting back to it because the next project has riveted their attention.
- They excel in managing details.
- They do well in middle management positions and can even rise to the top in organizations when job descriptions, goals and projects are clearly defined.

Agenda for Growth

To make the most of their strengths and develop their soul potential, Ones, Twos and Sixes have to develop their thinking center.

- They enhance their lives by learning to think objectively

and linearly. By sorting out issues and dealing with one at a time, they create order out of confusion.

➤ They need to trust their own impressions and thinking processes. Dependent types are often armed with a clutch of conditional words and phrases that protect them from owning their ideas — kind of, sort of, maybe, possibly, probably, it depends. These words create a psychic comfort zone around their thoughts so that, just in case they are not right, they can justify changing their position and claim, at least to themselves, they never adhered to the other idea in the first place.

➤ Learning how to say directly what they feel, know and experience creates a new freedom in their lives. Then, they can make decisions and proceed.

➤ They grow by relying on their own inner vision and intuition. By looking to others and situations to evaluate life and set the agenda, they give away their power. When they look within for guidance, they often find an abundance of wisdom about life and the strength to live it.

➤ Because thinking is undeveloped in dependent types, they can't evaluate themselves and tend to be overcritical. As they take all factors into account in their evaluations and develop a more compassionate style, they find greater strength and vitality.

➤ The thinking center also sets boundaries, which is why dependent types aren't skilled in this field. Learning to consider the consequences of their decisions before they speak prevents the frantic schedules that result from overcommitment.

► By saying no and setting limits on their expenditure of time and energy, they create order in their lives and the lives of those around them.

By accomplishing this agenda, Ones, Twos and Sixes stabilize their active lives, finding fulfilling relationships and spiritual vitality.

THE AGGRESSIVE STANCE

Three types repress the feeling center, Threes, Sevens and Eights. This doesn't mean they don't have feelings or relationships. Rather, it means that while these types are often expressive, they aren't emotional. They dismiss their emotions and/or express feeling indirectly. Regarding relationships, either they have an ulterior motive for them or their greatest struggle is being intimate in them. By avoiding the difficulties found in relationships and the emotional life, they can focus on thought and action, which is the origin of their up-beat, positive and optimistic attitude.

The feeling center was wounded in childhood in these types so their ability to express feelings and connect emotionally is limited. Many even say they don't have the vocabulary to express feeling. They cover this deficiency by dodging direct personal questions so artfully that listeners don't know they have done so till the conversation is over. This tactic also protects their privacy, decreases outside expectations, and increases their personal freedom, which is one of their highest values.

Calling them aggressive doesn't imply they are physically offensive. Rather, it means their unconscious drive is to reshape people and situations the way they want them to be. If the personal dimension of life doesn't show up on their view screen, they can use their energy any way they want to. With the importance of emotion and relationships out of the picture, life becomes a matter of having control, impressing their ideas on others, accomplishment, drive and achievement.

Thus, to others they can come across as pushy, although they are relatively unaware of how others are recoiling from them. Generally, they are oblivious to the people, feelings or needs that might be in the way of their project. If others become vocal about the pain they inflict, aggressive types pay the price later. They can also flip off the incident with humor; these types frequently use humor as a protective shield to keep people at bay and smooth over rough spots in relationships. They can also respond with a comment like, "Why didn't you tell me you were feeling that way?" thus placing responsibility for hurt feelings on the other party.

Threes, Sevens and Eights have a future-orientation that disguises their weakness in forming personal relationships: that is, they don't have to relate in situations that don't yet exist. Threes focus on completing the next project and the list of goals beyond that. Sevens' attention is riveted to the next activity, which they are sure will be fun and exciting. Eights are preparing for the next crisis or struggle.

Strengths

▶ The aggressive types tend to have a lot of energy because the delicacy and vulnerability of the feeling center does not weigh them down.

▶ Life is not dull or boring around them, and they contribute a lot to the scene wherever they are.

▶ Secretly, they often feel that life and others are moving too slowly and it's up to them to bring zest into situations.

▶ They are usually outwardly expressive and personable, even though their inner attitude may be impersonal.

▶ They tend to understand the realities of life.

▶ With thinking and doing leading the way, they know how to plan and execute a project.

▶ When planning a project, their estimation of expenditure of time, money and resources is generally accurate. However, in verbalizing their projections, they often calculate an added cushion so that, if they can finish the project under deadline and budget, they improve their image and standing among others.

▶ The aggressive types are able to dismiss personal offenses more easily than others because the feeling center, which has its petty side, is not dictating their responses. Their attitude is, "Why dwell on the past? Let's get on with life. There have to be more important things to do than to hold a grudge and wait for apologies."

► They are optimistic. Always looking to a better future, ready to take on the day's challenges, and assuming they will be able to achieve their goals, they create vitality and bring it to everyone in their lives.

Agenda for Growth

To make the most of their strengths and develop their soul potential, Threes, Sevens and Eights need to develop the feeling center.

► They enhance their lives when they slow down its pace. They can't experience emotions if they're living in the fast lane.

► Expressing emotion through art (as long as it does not become another "performance") can be a safer first step into the world of personal intimacy.

► Spending time with family and friends and in personal reflection will pay off in quality-of-life dividends.

► They improve their relationships by developing a feeling vocabulary and learning to value living at the feeling level.

► Initiating and remaining present to emotionally intimate communication supports their growth. Secretly, aggressive types often fear their emotions would overwhelm them and are sure they would overwhelm others. Because others have learned to depend on the aggressive types to be unemotional and take care of situations, they may indeed be shocked to discover the same range of emotion from fear to joy that others more easily express. However, people close to these types want and need to know how they feel.

▶ By paying more attention to other people's feelings and needs, they strengthen relationships.

To find healing, wholeness and spiritual depth, Threes, Sevens and Eights need to live in the security of friendship and family love that only comes with emotional intimacy.

THE WITHDRAWING STANCE

Three types have a repressed doing center, Fours, Fives and Nines. This doesn't mean they don't do anything. By observing the way they live, you may indeed conclude they are active people. But when you look closely at what they do, you discover they generally do what they like, not what needs to be done. In domestic projects, they are also tempted to take shortcuts rather than do a job the way it needs to be done. This can apply to any task from brushing their teeth to fixing the roof to painting the shelves in the garage.

Often, they are simply blind to the possibility they should do something about a situation. They'll wonder why it happened, analyze how it should be fixed, and suggest alternative solutions, but rarely do they take the initiative and do something about it. In simpler matters like seeing a piece of paper on the floor, they'll notice it and even be irritated because it is there, but walk right by it without even thinking to pick it up.

It's not that they think about what they could do and dismiss it. Rather, what they could do about the situation never crosses their minds.

Calling them the withdrawing types doesn't mean they're hopelessly introverted. Rather, it means they look within themselves for what they need. When they repress the ability to affect the world, a strength that comes with the doing center, they have to look within to survive.

With their doing center repressed, they lack confidence in connecting with the world. They can overcome this lack in various areas while still feeling hesitant or insecure in many hidden areas. They think and feel and talk more than they actually do. Generally facile with words, they are able to rationalize their way out of almost any difficulty.

Therefore, they live the interior life as if it were life in the real world, which can cause them to feel isolated from others and life. They can be dissatisfied with their lives because they don't know how to act on their own behalf. They also have difficulty moving their ideas through to completion.

All three types focus on the past because the doing center isn't needed there. Fours ruminate on relationships, conversations, and all that is missing from their lives. Fives think about information they have already gathered and from it fashion their own idea systems. Nines think about the way their lives were, both good and bad, and feel powerless to repair the bad or improve the good.

While many people respond well to nature, these types

often have a special affinity for the outdoors. They may or may not be sports minded, but the beauty and tranquillity of nature draws them to it.

Strengths

▶ These types appreciate intricacy and ponder life.

▶ Because they insightfully perceive the subtleties that underlie complicated ideas and interpersonal relationships, they often arrive at enlightened solutions. However, this same ability also causes them to consider themselves the final authority on anything important to them, and they can be condescending.

▶ They find life and people interesting.

▶ Often, they are good observers who notice and appreciate fine details others miss.

▶ They usually have a point of view that takes into account many factors overlooked by others, which makes them interesting people with whom to interact.

▶ The interplay between the thinking and feeling centers makes them inventive and creative people who are always looking for new ways to do things.

▶ They easily assimilate ideas and can synthesize different idea systems into new perspectives that benefit many. However, if they become self-involved with this process, they can become lost in their own thinking, create nothing of use, and have only the satisfaction of their unique perspective as the product of their thinking.

189

▶ When they don't withdraw to live only inside themselves, they are charming conversationalists.

▶ Although they can put on tough masks like anyone, they tend to be more gentle than rough.

▶ In difficult situations they are either affable or accommo-dating, though they may carry an underlying resentment if they do n't speak up for themselves.

Agenda for Growth

To make the most of their strengths and develop their soul potential, Fours, Fives and Nines need to develop the doing center.

▶ They can notice what needs to be done and do it the way it should be done without being asked. These things can range from picking up the pop can on the coffee table and taking it to the recycle bin to providing regular mainte-nance for their automobile.

▶ Learning to think practically and in consideration of the physical world around them improves the quality of their lives.

▶ When it comes to estimating time, money and resources for a project, the withdrawing types tend to underesti-mate. Because their thinking center has not been trained to observe the physical world, they are unaware of the many pitfalls one can encounter in completing a task.

▶ They can underestimate certain situations — for example, how long it will take to get from here to there — and then feel caught off guard when their predictions turn out to be inadequate.

▶ They can also overestimate other kinds of situations — the square footage of a new house or the number of people who attended an occasion.

▶ When a job is their sole responsibility, they can become discouraged and pessimistic, dramatically overestimating how long it will take to complete it, feel paralyzed and never begin the task.

▶ Their problems regarding practical thinking can be solved by developing the objectivity of the thinking center and teaching it to work in tandem with qualities from the doing center.

▶ They devise enlightened solutions and enhance their lives by putting these solutions into practice. Then they experience the satisfaction found in accomplishment.

▶ They also can learn to speak up and stand up for themselves. The assertive quality of the doing center has lain dormant for many years. Withdrawing types may "blow up" when they feel pressured or criticized, but they don't know how to consistently stand their ground day after day. Developing this kind of inner strength goes a long way in creating a sense of confidence and pride.

As they complete this agenda, Fours, Fives and Nines learn how to be fully involved in life and experience dynamic relationships and spiritual stamina.

Innocence and Greatness

One way to view the repressed center is that it stopped normal development somewhere between the ages of eight and 12. Therefore, a delightful surprise awaits you when you develop your repressed center. Since this center has been hidden away for protection, it does not bear the scars of dealing with the world. This is the most pure aspect of your inner life and, when you begin using it, you discover the most innocent and beautiful qualities of your soul.

For example, Kathy finds that as Theodorre (who is a Four) develops his repressed doing center, he is willing to extend himself graciously in service to the family in ways she would (as a Three) only with resistance. Similarly, Theodorre finds Kathy giving generous interpretations to other people's faults in the same situations he is tempted to be critical or intolerant. We are also aware of dependant types whose insight into situations is penetrating and clear as they choose to develop and trust their repressed thinking center.

Thus, if you want to stay young at heart, if you long to experience some of the innocence of childhood, develop your repressed center.

The life of the soul awaits you as you develop the center you use least well. Your soul becomes more open and receptive to the limitless love and power of the divine. Everything you do to develop your repressed center is a step on *your* inner quest to becoming a "great soul."

CHAPTER 4

SOUL EXPANSION:
BECOMING SPIRITUALLY ALIVE

"The fact that you are not dead is not sufficient proof that you are alive."
— Brother David Stendl-Rast

The date was February 28, 1995. The day before, we had driven from Denver through a treacherous blizzard to reach the little town of Lennox, South Dakota, which would be the final resting place of our beloved Grandma Hurley. On this morning, we were relieved to see that the storm-filled skies had cleared through the night, and the sun was now shining brightly.

During the winter in South Dakota, however, the bright sun does not necessarily mean warmer temperatures. It was 20 degrees below zero, and the wind made it feel much colder We quickly realized we were ill prepared to stand out in the open countryside where the cemetery was located.

After the service, as we waited in the vestibule of the church before beginning the drive to the grave side services, the funeral director pointed to a rack of warm coats and jackets he had gathered from his family and friends for us to use. As we gratefully put the coats on, we were humbled realizing these weren't old spare coats and jackets. People we had never met before had given us only their best and newest outerwear.

The cemetery was about ten miles from town. As the funeral procession moved slowly along the country road, we felt deeply touched by the respect shown as every car we encountered pulled over to the side of the road and stopped until the last car in our procession had passed. In the city, most funeral processions are barely tolerated because no one wants to get a traffic ticket. What was happening here shocked us into a new awareness of how easy it is to fall asleep, to be unconscious to the only things in life that really matter — namely, human kindness and respect for all that is sacred in life.

About half way along the route, we experienced how deeply our actions can affect others. A pickup truck stopped and an old rancher got out, took off his cowboy hat, placed it over his heart, and stood with head bowed in the freezing cold and sharp wind. The people who gave us their coats and the rancher who stopped to respect the life of a stranger dispelled the illusion that we were just a few people alone on a wind-swept prairie, grieving the loss of a woman we loved. Whether in life or in death, we are one with all creation.

Embracing Our True Selves

The Enneagram shows us how we are one by describing

human nature as nine variations of thinking, feeling and doing acting together in different proportions. It acts as a mirror that shows what is most true about ourselves. It gives us a structure by which to understand our inner lives. Instead of experiencing our inner selves as a set of random events, we are able to view them as emanating from the one of the three centers. This perspective helps us to respect every inner movement. These categories give us a way to sort, analyze, apply appropriate principles, and effect change.

This system empowers because it is based on the truth of our human nature. As you choose to understand and experience yourself through the lens of this truth, you experience yourself in a new way. Then you can create a new reality within that respects and upholds all that is good.

Learning and Loving the Enneagram

The first key is found in *learning* the Enneagram well enough to use it. Keeping knowledge in our heads allows us to pretend we are learning even as we defend ourselves against applying the knowledge for growth. We can study the Enneagram as an abstract, objective system, and it will fascinate us and provide great insight. However, this knowledge will change our lives permanently only when we allow it to enter our hearts, where we come to know that not only is it objectively true but also that it is true *for me*. Then it can flow into action and change our lives.

The second key is *loving* the wisdom the Enneagram

uncovers. The wisdom is not in the Enneagram; it is in ourselves. The Enneagram leads us to it. Loving that wisdom, however, means we apply it even when it asks us to give up long-standing attitudes about ourselves and life.

Many people are excited about the new life that comes from personal growth until they realize they have to give up some cherished attitudes to attain it. Their beliefs can be either positive or negative, self-condemning or self-justifying — it doesn't matter. What does matter is that they stop growth by locking us into our present state. When we question and search from a place of openness, we free ourselves from lifelong automatic patterns so we can begin to see ourselves and life from a deeper perspective.

The Enneagram challenges us to think for ourselves, not to think what we've been told to think; to feel and express our true emotions, not to feel what we've been conditioned to feel; to examine what we believe and why we believe it, not to believe what we've been told to believe; to do what we truly know is right for us, not to do what everyone else may be doing.

Living by old unexamined attitudes continues an unconscious, accidental life. In this state, we wander through an existence that others think we should live rather than spread our wings, soar to new heights and, carried on the strong currents of Spirit, gain a new perspective. *We can create the life we were meant to live.* Only by living intentionally can we cooperate with the mystery of our unfolding destiny and release the potential of our God-given soul power into the world.

The Third Key: Developing the Silent Witness

Viewing ourselves and life more perceptively depends on the ability to be objective. If we gain a new insight into ourselves but use it to judge ourselves or justify ourselves, it no longer can support our growth. The insight fades and becomes a part of the existing value system that has made us who we already are.

For example, through the Enneagram Fours learn that they readily blame others for their problems. This attitude is so ordinary to them, they may actually never have heard themselves shifting responsibility for their problems onto other people's shoulders. While the Enneagram makes them conscious of this trait, they can use their new awareness to become depressed about it or ratify their belief that others, not they, are responsible for their pain. At either point, growth stops.

However, if we allow a new insight to rest gently on our minds, its energy can point us in a new direction. In the case of Fours blaming others, they can look anew at the situation and discover points in the process at which a new decision or outlook would create a different outcome. This is *living* the Enneagram, doing the kind of inner work that can change the way we live.

As children, we were not taught to remain objective about

ourselves, but rather to judge and justify ourselves. Furthermore, we learned these were good things to do. If our caregivers wanted to curb our behavior, they often judged us as "bad" and taught us to do the same. On the other hand, when we defended our behavior against their judgments or when they defended our behavior against other people's criticism, we were simultaneously learning how to justify ourselves and discovering the vocabulary to do so. We were told these were normal reactions to have so they became part of the backdrop against which we play out our lives.

Judging and justifying ourselves both have the effect of short circuiting our efforts to change because, in either case, the energy created by the new insight drains away. Instead of putting our strength into changing, it goes into judging and feeling guilty, or into justifying and feeling entitled. These feelings only engage our egocentricity and keep us the way we are.

Gaining a new insight into ourselves or life retains its force for personal transformation only when we take it in objectively. The objective part of us acts like a silent witness that sees and records an historical event. At the same time, it is silent because it makes no judgments for or against what it sees. This is the third key to creating the new life the Enneagram offers.

The Silent Witness (sometimes called Observing I, the Observing Self or the Inner Observer) is a part of every person's consciousness, although in most people it is weak because it is rarely used. As it becomes stronger, a person can draw on its power to be an agent of change. It creates an awareness of what takes place in the moment and opens an inner space in which we discover we are always free to make different choices.

Because the Enneagram reveals many new insights meant to make us aware of how we get stuck in habitual responses to life, it is of ultimate importance we develop the Silent Witness within as we learn this system. Otherwise, we will see much of our efforts wasted as we use the Enneagram to judge and/or to justify ourselves.

When people are exposed to the Enneagram on a superficial level and don't learn it with both the head and the heart, don't use the wisdom when it challenges their attitudes and beliefs, and never develop the Silent Witness, the Enneagram too easily becomes a weapon used against themselves and others. They stereotype, judge, and too quickly categorize people as this or that type based on a few salient qualities. They don't look for the deeper unconscious motivation. Then, they may lose interest in the Enneagram because it isn't adding anything positive to their lives. Or they keep it in their heads where it entertains but does not provoke real change.

Accessing Inner Wisdom for Your Future

Wisdom often comes from the least expected source; as the saying goes, "From out of the mouths of babes. . . ." This truth can make discovering wisdom difficult. Without wisdom there can be no future worth living, for wisdom is the basis for improving the present. That's why it's important to develop the source of your inner wisdom — it is the fountain of your future.

The Enneagram teaches that the source of your inner wisdom — and the key to your future — lie in developing your repressed center of intelligence, the least expected source.

Personality is both a strength and a weakness. Personality is necessary because it is the vehicle by which we express ourselves in the world. When we express personality positively, it is the source of the good things that happen. Personality is constructively manifested when our three centers are balanced; this state allows soul to shine through into daily life.

However, personality can also be expressed negatively. Negative expressions of personality first limit our perspective and consequently our choices. They arise from the ways we misuse our three centers of intelligence.

The three centers get stuck in a pattern of interacting in a certain way that produces predictable results. The dominant center gives marching orders to the support center and squashes the involvement of the repressed center by dismissing its value. As a result, we have a limited set of responses at our disposal and can't see any possibility of expanding our repertoire, so we apply these responses whether or not they fit the situation.

We couldn't function in the world without personality.

From a more important point of view, we need personality because we have a responsibility to leave this world better than we found it.

The difficulty occurs when personality gets stuck in patterned reactions. This is the compulsive dimension of personality, or what is called false personality or the false self. False personality comprises all of our nonproductive and non-helpful ways of living.

The descriptions of the nine Enneagram types in chapter 2 revealed how negative personality traits originate in the overuse of one center of intelligence. It showed how your weaknesses are often really overused strengths. The wisdom for your future comes from developing your repressed center so your strengths won't have to be overused.

The Centers in Lockstep

It's easy to see how none of the three centers of intelligence are being used properly when you identify with your Enneagram type. Overly identified with your dominant intelligence, you overwork it, asking it to respond to situations for which it is not qualified. Then it draws on a few qualities of the support intelligence to augment its effectiveness, while the repressed intelligence sabotages everything by controlling the entire show from the unconscious.

Consequently, thinking is rote and opinionated, feeling is dominated by petty and misguided emotions, and actions are misdirected. And then we wonder why life seems so difficult and relationships fall apart, and we waste so much time and energy. This state is summarized best by the Chinese proverb, "If we do not change our direction, we are likely to end up where we are going."

Balancing Through Inclusion

Here, we come to a major breakthrough that occurs when we see the nine Enneagram types as nine different composites of the three centers in different proportions. "Balancing through inclusion" means you rectify the exaggerations created by the wrong use of centers (that produce your Enneagram type) by including the gifts, strengths and talents that, until now, have been missing from your life.

When people accept their Enneagram types, their usual first response is to attempt to rub off its rough edges. If they think they're too emotional, they try to be more self-contained; if they come on too strong, they pull back. In this "way of reduction" they try to *make themselves less of who they are.*

Instead, balancing through inclusion is a "way of expansion" by which you can become *less of who you are* not *and more of who you really are!* You expand your horizons by developing qualities, attributes and levels of appreciation you never experienced before. You take life in a new way as you do things you never thought you could do.

Your old self was convinced you didn't have the abilities you needed to be happy and successful. Now you realize these abilities were only hidden from your view; what blocked your vision was your Enneagram compulsion. With the development of these new gifts, many of the problems you used to experience slowly disappear while others become more manageable.

The Right Use of Centers

If all three centers are misused when we are in the grip of our Enneagram compulsion, we must learn to use them correctly and reclaim their hidden gifts. But immediately we come upon a major stumbling block. We have been saying all along our ordinary experience of the centers is the lower side of their potential. How do we know what to look for when searching for the gifts of the higher side?

The next pages present the three centers as they are intrinsically, not as they are misused. By presenting the centers in words and phrases, these pages offer the freedom of personal study and use of intuition so you can find your own relationship to these three intelligences of your soul.

THE THINKING CENTER

True Purpose
Vision; breadth and depth of awareness of the true meaning of reality.

Ordinary Use
Thinking, planning, abstracting, objectifying.

Natural Resources
- *New ideas*: inventiveness.
- *Possibilities*: making the unimaginable attainable.
- *Unrealized concepts*: discovering humanity's hopes and dreams.
- *Spiritual dimension*: ideals, values.
- *Pondering*: interconnections between seen and unseen.
- *Mystical unveiling of Truth*: "I am the Truth."

The Center of Initiation: Symbols and Images
- The Spirit of God.
- The mystery of overshadowing.
- Breath.
- Seed and potential.
- Season: Spring.
- Flowing water: it can't be captured, except in the imagination.

The Intelligence of Vision: Symbols and Images
- The eye.
- The inner eye.
- The Mastery of this intelligence is consciousness.
- This center is the receptive home of divine light.

204

The Feeling Center

True Purpose

Connectedness, healthy and wholesome relationship with self, others, the universe, and God.

Ordinary Use

Expression of emotions, relationships, interpersonal dynamics.

Natural Resources

- *Incarnation*: making the intangible tangible.
- *Synthesizing*: combining diverse concepts into a whole.
- *Integrating*: uniting random knowledge into new systems.
- *Spiritual intuition*: the cry for freedom in the human heart.
- *Spiritual perception*: perceiving deeper realities in people.
- *Desire for the Good*: "I am the Way."

The Center of Manifestation, Epiphany: Symbols and Images

- The Divine Healer.
- The mystery of redemption.
- Artist.
- Planting and growing.
- Season: Summer.
- Fire: spiritual energy of mysticism and transformation.

The Intelligence of Union: Symbols and Images

- The ear.
- The inner ear.
- The mastery of this intelligence is process.
- This center is the receptive home of divine love.

THE DOING CENTER

True Purpose
Guidance, intent and energy needed to complete the work of being a person in the world.

Ordinary Use
Safety, reacting, accomplishment, movement.

Natural Resources
- *Freedom*: expressing one's true nature.
- *Guidance*: sense of timing regarding how to accomplish.
- *Development*: stage-by-stage advancement for progress.
- *Completion*: actualizing concepts.
- *Access to the material world*: ease with material reality.
- *Innovation creating the Beautiful*: "I am the Life."

The Center of Creation: Symbols and Images
- The Divine Creator.
- The mystery of nurturing.
- Presence.
- Harvest and festival.
- Season: Autumn.
- Earth: source of life, home of death, rich in resources.

The Intelligence of Actualization: Symbols and Images
- Mouth, hands and feet.
- Inner locution.
- The mastery of this center is creative expression.
- This center is the receptive home of divine life.

Surprises from the Centers

As we have worked with this material over the years, each center has yielded many surprises. These grander potentialities cause us to muse on the exhilarating possibilities of human nature and the common work of the human race as we develop our soul potential.

The thinking center. Because our culture overvalues the thinking center, we are most familiar with its strengths. Still, we delightedly recognize it as the origin of all change. Every new thing begins with an idea. Even personal transformation begins with an image of ourselves as a different person.

We were also gratified to find this center to be the home of faith and trust. While trust and knowing are not the same, there is a relationship between the two. Trust is not blind; you must know some things about someone before you can trust him or her. Then trust is the leap of inner knowing beyond factual knowing. As an extension of comprehension, trust is the transcendental expression of the thinking center.

The feeling center. The feeling center is the home of synthesis, conscience and will. It is about relationships, but not only personal ones. Synthesis is establishing new relationships among ideas, images or emotions. Conscience establishes the relationship between ourselves and ethical values.

It took us a while to understand why will is a part of this center. Realizing that every emotion has its own "little will" was the key. The little wills of emotions drag us in one direction and then in another when our emotions control our lives.

Then our sense of will is fragmented and we become inconsistent and undependable. One of the most exalted goals of inner work is to recognize the many little wills that run our lives and to tame them so that they all desire one object. The person who has a single will, all the emotions magnetized in the same direction, is a fully conscious being.

The doing center. When we first learned the Enneagram, much of the commentary about the doing center seemed overly ponderous. That's why we were especially excited to discover it is the home of harvest and festival, joy and delight, creation, beauty and guidance.

Doing in part is movement, which in part is play and dance. With joy and delight on the high side and pleasure seeking on the low side, we understand this center's intertwining with human experience; it creates an interface between us and material reality. Everything is created when the doing center gently holds the fruits of thinking and feeling to manifest them. Beauty results from manifestation. Guidance results from applying the wisdom of the feeling and thinking centers working together.

This center wonderfully contains wisdom about when *not* to do. It is not only the intelligence of accomplishment but also of rest, not only productivity but also creative leisure, not only doing but also being. Awareness of this hidden side of the doing center (at least hidden to our western First World culture) expands our understanding of it so it can take its rightful place as an equal beside the other two.

The Wisdom of the Three Centers of Intelligence

Used ordinarily, the centers of thinking, feeling and doing work in automatic, habitual patterns. We've become so accustomed to living as less than who we were created to be that we fear and resist the possibility of becoming who we really are.

One of the most subtle ways we justify our choice not to change is by wearing the mask of false humility: "It would be prideful of me to believe that God has a great purpose for my life." How often we use God to excuse our apathy and laziness!

Similarly, knowing your Enneagram type can be used to justify yourself and blame others for causing the pain in your life. Or, understanding your Enneagram type can be the gateway into exploring the heights and depths, length and breadth of your soul.

What prevents us from discovering the wonder of who we really are? Nelson Mandela described it well in his 1994 inaugural speech as president of South Africa:

> It is our light, not our darkness, that most frightens us. . . . We were born to make manifest the glory of God that is within us. It is not just in some of us, it is in everyone. And as we let our own light shine, we give others permission to do the same. As we are liberated . . . our presence automatically liberates others.

The time to become all that you were created to be is now. The point of entry is where you are. All that you need you already possess. Just begin.

CHAPTER 5

SOUL HEALING
AND SPIRITUAL VITALITY

*"As a human being is part of the whole, called
by us "Universe" — a part limited in time and
space. He experiences himself, his thoughts and
feelings, as something separate from the rest —
a kind of optical delusion of his consciousness.
This delusion is a kind of prison for us, restricting
us to our personal desires and to affection for a few
persons nearest to us. Our task must be to free
ourselves from this prison by widening our circle of
compassion to embrace all living creatures and to
the whole of nature in its beauty."*
— Albert Einstein

Throughout this book, we've written about the unavoid-
able wounding that takes place in everyone's life. The French
word *blessure,* means both wounding and blessing, expressing
a connection between the two experiences. Since no one gets
through life unscathed, and since the wound you experience
is expressed as your Enneagram type, the question becomes,

"How can I turn the pain of my life into blessing?"

It is our belief that, alone, we are unable to heal our wounds and turn them into blessings. It's obvious that if techniques, analysis, therapy, programs or information could heal a wounded heart or a wounded soul, everyone would be healed. Something more is needed. Love is the primal healing energy. God — called by whatever name you use to describe the divine Source of life — is love and therefore the source of all healing.

From the time we first learned the Enneagram almost 20 years ago, we applied its insights to the process of healing the human soul. Soul development depends on healing, and knowing your type becomes a guide on your journey of healing. One of the gifts of the Enneagram is that it details specific and different needs for healing in each of the nine types.

Over the last several decades, our culture has experienced a growing awareness of the nature and process of healing. Consequently, there exist many approaches to healing, and a myriad of philosophies, theologies and technologies that claim to produce various kinds of healing.

When it comes to soul healing or spiritual healing practices, many people carry one of two attitudes. Some believe all healing is self-healing, that the created universe contains many spiritual energies both known and unknown, and healing results from connecting with or harnessing these energies for self-improvement.

Others believe in God and think that God does all the

healing. All we need do is ask, or obey God's laws, or follow some religious practice that places us in God's favor, and healing will happen magically.

In this chapter, we want to explore a third option. That is the world of "*blessure*," a world in which wounds become blessings.

How Do Wounds Become Blessings?

Our world is immense, diverse and unpredictable. Some people in it are good, others are not. On the one side, we see beauty in nature, wonder in the innocence of children, and contentment in fulfilling relationships. On the other side, systems, structures and institutions create the context of our lives but often seem to have little regard for the people who depend on them. The world is too complex to be dependable.

To find healing, we must be secure enough to reveal our weaknesses. How do we experience the security that forms the basis of healing in an undependable and insecure world?

Only belief in some Higher Power, Higher Being or Higher Influence creates a context for healing. Without belief that someone more powerful than ourselves loves us, we will forever be suspicious of others and of life. So asking God for healing through prayer is necessary.

Because we have been given free will, God does not usually take part in our process until invited to do so. Prayer is our request and love is the response. Thus, prayer is the first step. But equally important are our practical efforts to cooperate with the grace it bestows.

Following this path, we also discover where and how we prevent our own healing. Suspicion of others, unwillingness to surrender, and unwillingness to choose love instead of imposing our ideas on ourselves and others — these attitudes create the roadblocks that prevent divine love from entering and healing from taking place. These areas thus become our personal agendas for spiritual growth and soul development.

Healing Is a Process of Hope

In this day of instant everything in the material world, sometimes it's difficult to accept the fact that the most important spiritual realities take time to unfold. So it is with healing. As the Dalai Llama said, "Those who believe in instantaneous healing have experienced a psychological collapse."

Healing is a process, and life is the process of the soul's development. The process of soul healing yields hope, for life is bland if what we are living now is all that is meant to be with no possibility of improvement.

Hope is completely different from wishful thinking. When we wish kind things for self and others, our thoughts are fanciful and insubstantial because they have no basis in reality. The hope contained in healing is based on the reality of God and the reality of the three centers within us, which express the three prime qualities of God: truth, goodness and beauty; or thought, feeling and action. Tangled with each other in the state of Enneagram compulsion, the centers create egocentricity. Freed from each other to express their true identity, they access our true selves. Life-giving energy emanates from them.

Embracing the Enneagram Compulsion

The process of hope we call healing is founded on an experience that seems to be its opposite: facing the darkness within. If we can't face our weaknesses and faults, we run from them and in running we make them our enemies. Then we fight and attempt to obliterate this enemy, which is only ourselves expressed in ways we don't like or can't accept.

Some of the greatest evil in history has been perpetrated by those who desired to eliminate evil. Although at first it seems honorable to want to destroy evil, when we examine this attitude more closely, we realize it is violent. Violence begets violence. We must find another way.

This is not only true in the history of this planet, the macrocosm; it is also true in the microcosm of our inner lives. Violence begets violence, and so violent approaches to personal transformation yield nothing positive, even when they seem to do so at first glance. Their ultimate result is negative: to disrespect, to divide and to destroy.

That's why, when it comes to the insight the Enneagram gives us for healing, the first step is to embrace the compulsion, to embrace the negative as well as the positive qualities detailed by the Enneagram. So often our first reaction to these negative qualities is to deny or avoid them. We convince ourselves we've faced that problem and dealt with it already. We twist our perceptions to believe we never had that problem in the first place. We do battle with the qualities we dislike and, for a time, believe we have overcome them.

The truth is, if we seek to reclaim our souls, we must begin with the dark side of our human nature. This dark side is but an expression of the wounded essential self or soul. Encountering the evil embodied in our Enneagram passion is crucial in integrating and reclaiming both the fullness and unity of soul.

The most powerful enemy is the one we're unaware of. By ignoring or avoiding the passion that names our pain so accurately, we trade our soul potential for surface, ephemeral comfort. On the other hand, by embracing the compulsion, we create the possibility of discovering the treasure buried in the field, the gift in the pain, the world of *blessure*. We create the possibility of inner unity. We move *through* the compulsion to the truth, goodness and beauty of the three centers, and then to the soul.

The Passion As Wound

In chapter 2, we described a "formula" for each of the passions named in the Enneagram. Each of the passions — anger, pride, deceit, envy, greed, fear, gluttony, lust and sloth — is the core of one of the Enneagram types.

As we examine this list, we realize these qualities are shared by humanity in general. One of the marks of genius in the Enneagram is that, while it acknowledges these are weakness common to all people to one degree or another, one is the foundation of each person's ego. Early in life, because of our perception of our childhood wounding and not having our needs met, the centers constellate around one of these passions. It becomes the lens through which we see self, others, life, the world and God until we choose to become conscious.

Sometimes, we experience this passion-wound as an emptiness that hurts when it is touched. At other times, it operates as a defense to keep us from feeling vulnerable, afraid or alone. However we experience it, it deceives us. It keeps us from seeing reality objectively by convincing us that we and the world are enemies, even that we and God are enemies.

This passion-wound causes disfigurement of the emotional or feeling center. All people have greatest difficulty with the feeling center because it is the seat of the egocentric ego. The feeling intelligence personalizes reality and therefore creates our subjective view of it. Being the opposite of objective consciousness (which is the equivalent of seeing the way God sees) subjective consciousness is our most obvious obstacle on the road to soul healing. It is the fountain from which flows all the reasons we think life should go our way. It maintains the illusion that life owes us something and we have the right to push and shove and stomp and fight to get it. It keeps us from being vulnerable to love.

Objective Prayer

Healing for this passion-wound begins in prayer. We look at ourselves objectively, identifying the thoughts and feelings that led to our reaction. This inner work is the most basic form of prayer. In it, our knowledge of our Enneagram type can be of great help, for it points to our favorite ways of defending ourselves and projecting responsibility onto others. This mirror does not lie. However, self-observation alone doesn't heal. Rather, it paves the way for healing.

With our observations consciously named, we can rest more securely in our souls that know goodness, beauty and truth. Our souls especially know God and the reason for our existence. Here, we surrender to God feelings of hurt and thoughts of retaliation and defensiveness. Instead, we consciously intend to allow God to handle matters. Then we can be open to experiencing a taste of love and to participate in forgiveness as necessary.

Understanding our passion as wound is important. Otherwise, we too easily blame ourselves for the wound, fight it, attempt to hide it, or make it seem "nicer" to ourselves and others so we won't feel exposed. When we accept ourselves as wounded but not flawed, we widen the circle of compassion within ourselves. This movement then allows us to widen our circle of compassion in the world till we know the mind and heart of God.

We move along this path by combining the inner experiences of self-observation, remembering who we are, and choosing to do our work in the presence of God. This is the most basic meaning of prayer.

Prayer, love and soul are traditional words commonly used in religious and spiritual circles. They have often been interpreted with pietistic and moralistic overtones that obscure their real purpose. However, they have specific objective meanings in the context of developing your soul potential by using the Enneagram.

Prayer cannot be effective when it is pietistic or moralistic. These attitudes engage the ego or Enneagram compulsion. Pietism overly emphasizes the emotional and personal religious response; when applied to prayer, it romanticizes prayer into a self-delusional state. Moralism creates the dualistic thinking of good versus bad, right versus wrong, that leads to self-righteousness.

In a state of authentic prayer, we remember who we really are — one, loving, tranquil, strong. We experience our sense of self in soul, not in ego. This can happen only when the three centers of intelligence cooperate with each other freely. Thus, our Enneagram type describes the state of egocentric ego. To the degree we disentangle the three centers and develop each for its true purpose, we are able to pray objectively.

In prayer, we first objectively look at our selves from the point of view of the Silent Witness, without self-condemnation or self-justification. The key to self-observation lies in the word *self*. We tend to be skilled in observing the short-comings of others but are quite blind to our own faults until we begin this process.

Then, we disengage from all thought and feeling that is not love. We do this in the presence of God's love for us and as a way of responding in love in return. This process often isn't easy or simple. In fact, it can be a great struggle.

Disengaging From the Ego's Resistance

The ego clings, attaches and desires; this is the source of our suffering. The ego holds on to pain. It says, "I'm hurt by what you did" or "I'm offended by what happened." Then it justifies itself and condemns others, or it condemns itself and exonerates others. Either way, blame creates the illusion that pain is our lot in life and nothing can be done about it.

But the ego believes what it does is good because we have little experience of anything different. We live by habit. The Enneagram reveals how our three centers of intelligence operate in rigid, habitual ways. Someone once described insanity as continually doing the same thing in the same way and expecting different results. Until we wake up and become conscious, our unconscious patterns of behavior perpetuate the pain we experience. Only by becoming aware of these patterns will we ever change and healing happen.

The Enneagram shows we have great potential to be different. This is our soul potential, but we have to disengage from the ego's resistance to find this inner "more real" self that knows love, peace and joy.

In this process, we are freed of the negative traits

described by our Enneagram compulsion one at a time. Little by little, our sense of self disengages from the egocentric ego and comes to rest in the soul. Our soul remembers why we were created and how we are to serve.

Our ego believes life owes us; it projects blame onto people and situations outside us. Our soul knows that we owe life because everything is a gift, especially life itself.

Brian Swimme said, "The universe is an inexhaustible expression of ultimate mystery." We require objective prayer to reconnect with the mystery.

Conscious Love

Just as prayer cannot be effective when it is pietistic, neither can love. Religious or spiritual love of God is often misinterpreted as an emotional swelling of the heart at hearing the name of God. It is also often thought to be the motivation to do good deeds. Love between two human beings is often misinterpreted as emotional attachment that then justifies a series of demands, dependencies and ego-gratifications. We project our desires, needs, and even our problems on the one we say we love. We expect another to fulfill us. When we feel unfulfilled, we easily become hurt, jealous, mean-spirited and spiteful.

About 150 years ago, an obscure Russian monk named Theophan, who would later be recognized as the force behind the renewal of monastic life for the Russian Orthodox religion, was searching for a new word to express his understanding of true love or divine love. The word he coined was "consciousness." He said that true love is not blind. It is supremely aware, objectively aware. God is objectively aware of all creatures, and this is the nature of God's universal and unconditional love for all creatures. God sees creation as it is. From God's objective viewpoint, all is beautiful, all is wonderful, all is good, because all proceeds from God, who is love.

Many people today use the word "consciousness" to name the goal of their lives but do not recognize its original spiritual roots. They write and talk about consciousness as if it were some abstract state of a rarified intellect and not the product of a purified heart, a heart brimming with the recognition of the goodness of all creatures. On the other side, there are many religious people who, without knowing the origin and true meaning of the word, reject consciousness as a goal of the spiritual life. They even believe it distracts from the life goals toward which their religion directs them. On both sides, the cause of true love is not served.

True love of God is expressed in the journey of soul development, for the soul remembers who we really are. We are good, whole and pure by nature. The first half of our purpose in life is to become healed so we can express our true nature. Then we can be agents of healing in the world. This is our service to humanity. This is the world of *blessure.*

In other words, life is not about what we do day-to-day, it's about *who we become* as we do what we do. Life is about creating life, not about having our egocentric needs met.

In our families, friendships and associations with others, we enhance our lives by recognizing that, if we live unconsciously (that is, unlovingly), we create tangled webs of projections and expectations and call them relationships. Or as John Bradshaw say, we don't have relationships, we take hostages. We see in others the problems we ourselves possess. We expect others to take care of our needs so we can feel good because of what the other person gives us.

The Enneagram supports us in identifying our weaknesses so we can disentangle our lives from others' and take responsibility for ourselves and our reactions to people and to life. We learn we don't react this way or that because of what other people say or do, but because we choose to remain unconscious of our power to change automatic reactions into caring responses. By gaining a more objective view of other people, life and ourselves, we participate in the creation of love.

Love's Expression Is Service

If our personal lives are to have meaning and our communal life is to advance toward God and the fulfilment of the universe's purpose, more than living our daily lives is required of us. We are meant to serve and even endure suffering for a good greater than ourselves.

Living to satisfy our wants and desires is meaningless and narrow. Living to serve the future creates meaning and purpose. We each have the responsibility to serve the future without expecting anything in return.

One of the most natural ways people fulfill this responsibility is by raising children. Those who rear their children to respect others and creation, to take responsibility for their actions, to maximize their talents, and to make a contribution to life often sacrifice a great deal to advance these ideals.

On the other side, the tragedy of child neglect, child abuse, warehousing children for 12 or more hours a day in day care, and lack of setting appropriate limits for children with appropriate consequences creates a devolution of society. As parents deflect the responsibilities of child rearing, they not only lose their main opportunity to serve the future, they also diminish the possibility of their own soul development.

These reflections on child rearing are but an example of how everything depends on other things to maintain its existence. We depend on the resources of the earth to sustain life. How do we repay the earth? We depend on many other people for the food, shelter, clothing, love and inspiration we experience in life. How do we repay them?

Thus, service brings us to the inner conflict between generosity and selfishness. The Enneagram is about nine different ways of being selfish, nine different ways of being egocentric, and nine different ways of attempting to gain control. Each type has its own strategy for serving its needs and keeping the rest of the world at arm's length. However, within each Enneagram type are many strengths to assist the person in unlocking generosity of heart and greatness of spirit. We only need desire to find them.

In the early 1940s, two great spiritual figures, George Gurdjieff and Teilhard de Chardin, saw a great process of spiritualization proceeding on the earth and throughout the solar system. They believed we each had to make our contributions to this process; we would accomplish this goal by the way we live our lives. When we realize everything and everyone is interconnected, it becomes apparent that the quest for soul healing is not simply a choice or even a personal freedom. Rather, it is a collective responsibility.

Redefining Forgiveness

Inevitably, as we live collectively and relate with others, people rub each other in the wrong way. At these times, it is easy to seek and find reasons to blame the other person for the problem. That's when giving and receiving forgiveness becomes crucial.

When we cloud our minds with expectations and assumptions, we believe we have a right to feel offended when people do things that hurt us. We feel justified in holding others accountable for how we feel. We judge and hold a grudge. By taking this spiritual stance, we feel slightly superior when we finally forgive the other party and resume normal relations.

When we disentangle our egocentric projections and needs from others and experience ourselves in our souls, we learn the art of participating in God's forgiveness, which is very different from what was described above. In the Christian scriptures, Jesus says, "Do not judge lest you be judged." The spiritual meaning of these words leads to the core of the forgiveness message.

When we judge others, we proclaim our wounds. We say, "You hurt me, and I'm angry at you for it." That shows we are protecting our wound. We are defending our right to be wounded and holding another accountable for touching the wound and hurting us. The ego clings to pain, using it as an excuse for not changing or growing. Therefore, when we judge others, we proclaim our unwillingness to surrender our wounds to God for healing.

God doesn't want to judge but rather to love and heal. However, to find God's love and healing, we have to find God. Throughout the Jewish and Christian scriptures, God identifies with the poor and disenfranchised. While we enrich our ego by claiming talents here and rights there, our wounds are poor and defenseless. God lives in our wound, waiting for us to leave identification with the egocentric ego and accept this poor, weak aspect of ourselves.

We find our wounds in many places within. The repressed center lies dormant because it is wounded. Our Enneagram passion — the core negative experience of our type — is created by a wound. The many wounds and reactions to wounds we have experienced in life blind us to our souls themselves.

As we embrace our wounded selves in love, we free God to activate love and heal us. Then there is no need to "forgive" the other person. We simply let go of the situation and the pain it holds.

In truth, it is the greatest spiritual arrogance to believe we can forgive another person. Only God can forgive. We participate in God's forgiveness of others by letting go of the pain they have caused.

Healing Is in Relationship

We are wounded in relationship. We are healed in relationship. There is no withdrawing to a magical sanctuary to find healing; only loneliness and illusion await us there. Ironically, it is out in the world mixing it up with people and with life that our inner selves find wholeness. Real peace and tranquillity result.

Gratitude grounds all healing. Gratitude for everything, not because you like it or it feels good, but because it exists. God is somewhere in it — loving, supporting, teaching, guiding, revealing, inspiring, hoping, connecting with you, and connecting you with self, others, all of creation and God's own divine being.

Gratitude is easy. In truth, forgiveness, kindness, love and any other virtue is easy. The test is consistency. Can I be consistently grateful, kind, loving and forgiving? This is the goal that creates happiness, and it is the very purpose for disentangling the three centers.

One cannot be grateful and unhappy at the same time. If I am consistently grateful both in and for all relationships, I must be consistently happy. My own happiness in life and in relationships is always in my power to choose.

To be grateful in all things requires viewing our lives from a spiritual perspective. On the natural plane, it feels normal to be upset when things don't go our way, to be angry and hurt when we are forgotten or ignored, to want to retaliate when we feel treated unjustly, to play victim instead of using real strength against abuse. Only from a spiritual perspective do all of life's experiences, both pleasant and unpleasant, find meaning and yield gratitude. This perspective doesn't minimize great tragedies; sometimes it takes more effort and grace to understand the spiritual meaning of tragic events.

Many people experience personal tragedy in the rejection or abandonment they feel from family members, especially parents. Other significant figures also can represent moments of alienation because they didn't believe in us when we needed it the most.

Yet, despite these experiences, we're still here. What created the resilience to maintain our selves and a least a part of our dignity so we could go on? Often it is others' rejection, abandonment, and lack of belief in us that makes us affirm and believe in ourselves. These negative experiences cause us to look deeper, draw on hidden strengths, and come up stronger as we live our lives. We consequently learned to relate more deeply with ourselves. We found other people with whom to relate, communicate and recreate our lives.

We are broken in relationship. We are healed in relationship. Everything is a gift. This may reveal what Thomas

Merton meant when he said, "God is not found outside ourselves." Brother David Stendl-Rast's reflection on these words is equally inspiring: "This is the most important theological statement of the twentieth century."

Spiritual Vitality Revealed

In late June of 1977, my (Kathy) best friend Rose and I were attending an annual retreat for women. We stayed in a small camper trailer we had brought with us because Rose was nursing her five-month-old baby. During the first night, I was awakened by a soft moaning sound. Because we were camped in the woods, I tried not to move a muscle as I listened intently for the sound I thought came from outside. Then it ceased.

Soon the moaning sound started again. This time, however, because I was now fully awake, I realized it came from inside the camper. In the midst of her obvious pain, I could hear Rose softly murmur, "Yes Lord, yes. Your will be done." I felt as if I had been caught eavesdropping on two lovers and, not knowing what to do, I remained silent and prayed God would take away her pain.

By morning, Rose was back to her happy, cheerful self. She never mentioned being in pain and acted so normal that I began to wonder if what I had heard had been my imagination or a dream. We attended all the morning activities, but after lunch Rose told me she was going to call her husband to come and get her because she wasn't feeling well.

Within a few days, my friend had an operation for

advanced colon cancer and soon after was given six months to live. She was twenty-nine years old. Immediately our prayer group began to pray for the miracle of healing. Rose lived for over four years, and during that time we saw miracle after miracle take place. Rose never experienced the debilitating side effects of chemotherapy, and until the last week of her life, she needed nothing more than Tylenol to relieve pain.

However, even as I watched it unfold, I didn't recognize the greatest miracle of all until nearly ten years after her death. In fact, when the miracle began to happen, I thought she was creating unnecessary pain for herself and told her so. She just laughed, thanked me for my concern and promised to stop if it became too difficult.

And what was this healing miracle? Rose began to look back over her life and make a list of all the people she had offended, detailing the ways she had offended them. She was intensely honest with herself as she recalled everything — an unkind word, a lie, a manipulation, an intentional cruelty, a thoughtless action, etc. Each time she became clear about how she had wronged another person, she would make contact by letter, phone or in person to admit her fault and ask forgiveness.

After completing that phase, Rose made a list of everyone who had influenced her life in a positive way. She noted how their kindness, encouragement or support had helped her grow on her life journey. Rose remembered everyone's kindness — grocery clerks, former bosses, teachers, neighbors, friends, clergy and family members, as well as the people who delivered her mail, repaired her car and removed her trash. She then contacted each of them and thanked them for the love they had given her.

Looking back, I am deeply grateful that, after my initial attempt to dissuade Rose from beginning this process, I put my energy into supporting her the best way I knew how. Sometimes my "best" was simply not verbalizing my desire to protect her from the sadness I saw when she remembered how her words or actions had hurt another person.

Rose was not a celebrity or a movie star, she never wrote a book, she never put herself forward in any way. She was a young wife and mother who loved her family and attended church and prayer meetings. She liked to bowl, play volley-ball, and invite friends over for a backyard barbeque in the summer or for laughter, love and a glass of wine in front of a roaring fire on cold winter nights. However, by embracing, in the presence of a loving God, the pain and struggles, joy and victories of her life, Rose entered the world of *blessure*, awak-ened her soul potential, and touched the hearts of people all over the world.

Rose died on August 13, 1981. It had been a cloudy, rainy afternoon and early evening. Yet, within minutes of her passing, the sun burst forth and gave birth to a spectacular double rainbow. So unusually intense in color and depth, the rainbows were the object of special study by the National Center for Atmospheric Research in Boulder, Colorado. They commanded the lead story on the 10 P. M. news that night and the front page headlines of both Denver newspapers the following day. Only her husband and a few of her closest friends knew that the rainbow was Rose's personal symbol of complete healing.

A few days later, seven priests joined to celebrate her funeral mass. The church, which has a seating capacity of 1100, was not large enough to accommodate the friends of this remarkable woman. People stood in the aisles, in the church vestibule, even in the parking lot.

During the last four years of her short life, Rose became a *mahatma* — "a great soul" — by living naturally what most people have had to read in books first to learn and then to live. *But we must read and we must live this wisdom.*

When we do, we will know our individual soul potential. Then, we will be able to recreate a world soul of love and healing. We will know that God does not live outside us, individually or collectively, and we will experience this simple yet remarkable description of what it means to be human.

IDEAS THAT SUPPORT
THE JOURNEY INWARD

"As is your sort of mind,
So is your sort of search;
you'll find
What you desire."

— Robert Browning

Words that create ideas access the divine. This glossary of words and phrases important to the message of this book will support people who want to live this work. May it be a feast for your heart, soul, mind and strength, so that you can love God and love your neighbor even as you love yourself.

Aggressive Stance. Three types repress the feeling center; they are the Three, Seven and Eight. They are aggressive in the sense that, deprived of the intelligence that would connect them to the feelings and needs of others as well as of themselves, they want to shape people and the world to be the way they want them to be.

Avoidance. Each Enneagram type revolves around an

uncomfortable feeling that the type attempts to avoid with another feeling it considers more soothing. The desire to avoid this feeling is the originating point for the compulsion because it fuels the passion.

Balancing Through Inclusion. When the nine types of the Enneagram of personality are seen one-dimensionally (that is, on the level of type alone), they present a false solution to the problem that type describes. When people recognize their type, they see many thought, feeling and behavioral patterns that are not helpful. In fact, they want to change them. The false solution is to pare down excesses, to become "less of who I am." No matter how well intentioned, this resolve is doomed to failure because at its core is a resolve to fight oneself, to do violence to oneself. However, when one's perception of the nine Enneagram types gains depth by acknowledging the configuration of centers that underlies and creates type, another more positive and creative solution emerges: include and develop the center that is repressed. By doing so, people acquire the gifts of the repressed center that, as they take their place in the person's life, alleviates the need to overuse the dominant center and the support center. In this way, the goal of transformation subtly shifts to becoming "more of who I really am and less of who I am not." The term "balancing through inclusion" originates in the Qabalah's (the Jewish mystical tradition) approach to spiritual growth.

Breakthrough Enneagram®. This innovative model of the Enneagram is based on a development of the ideas in Hurley and Donson's second book, *My Best Self: Using the Enneagram to Free the Soul* and is presented fully in this book. It depicts each type visually as its own composite of the three centers of intelligence — thinking, feeling and doing. It reveals the configuration of centers that underlies each passion. This understanding of the nine Enneagram types does not invalidate older and more traditional interpretations of the Enneagram; rather, it builds upon them. It explains how this system is not artificial arises directly from human nature. It welcomes all the insights the previous model gives about self and organizes them into the three everyday categories of how people think, feel and behave. It uniquely explains why there are nine and only nine types and why certain qualities are associated with one type and not with others. Most importantly, by describing type in a dynamic way as created by three misused centers, it gives the prescription for transformation even as it makes the diagnosis: balancing through inclusion.

Challenge. This is the goal for transformation for each type named as a unique quest for the soul through balancing the three centers of intelligence.

Compulsion. The nine Enneagram types are sometimes referred to as compulsions because they are each driven by a passion that the type feels compelled to carry out.

Compulsive Expression. People can access either the higher or lower expression of the qualities of their type. The compulsive expressions of each type is the lower expression because it is automatic and mechanical and therefore not free.

Configuration of Centers. In Hurley and Donson's presentation of the Enneagram of personality, the nine passions are created by nine unique configurations of the three centers of intelligence — thinking, feeling and doing. These configurations represent a ranked order of preference of the three centers. As information is being processed, or as a person tries to make sense out of life, one center is dominant, another supports the dominant center, and the third center is repressed. The nine types of the Enneagram result. Balancing through inclusion, a cornerstone of the Qabalah, (the Jewish mystical tradition) becomes the prescription for healing and the path to transformation.

Conscience. Conscience is a natural morality that is part of the feeling center. It is natural because the feeling center is created whole, without a negative side, so the sense of morality is complete though usually undeveloped. It is a part of soul. Then, through the process of maturation, people lose connection with soul as personality and false personality form. They generally spend most of their conscious energy in the false personality, which is identified with the cares and anxieties of the world. At this stage real conscience is buried. In its place is acquired conscience, which is the equivalent of Freud's superego. Its principles come from outside and are formed by the world. Acquired conscience is different in every person.

Convictions. When a person thinks for him- or herself, convictions are formed. You can tell the difference between your opinions and convictions by noticing when you feel offended. Convictions require no need for defense.

Core Strengths. Along with its blind spots or potential obstacles and its compulsion or passion, each type has developed remarkable strengths through life. By highlighting these strengths, the Enneagram supports each type in identifying the qualities that directly express their personhood or soul.

Dependent Stance. Three types repress the thinking center; they are the One, Two and Six. They are dependent in the sense that, deprived of the intelligence that would support them in thinking for themselves and setting their own agendas, they look outside themselves — to a person or group or to the situation — to see what should happen next.

Divine Image. At the core of each Enneagram type is an unblemished spark of the divine. These divine images come from the Hebrew mystical tradition called the Qabalah. The divine image for the One is Wisdom, for the Two is Understanding, for the Three is Love, for the Four is Power, for the Five is Beauty, for the Six is Endurance, for the Seven is Majesty, for the Eight is Foundation, and for the Nine is Presence. The passion is a distortion of the divine image. To the degree a person balances the three centers of intelligence, the divine image shines through.

Doing Center. The purpose of the doing center, sometimes called the instinctive-moving center, is intent and enactment, knowing when and how to accomplish, and knowing when and how to rest. The most helpful functions of this center include guidance, inventiveness and joy. But when people are caught in their Enneagram compulsion, it operates mostly in the realm of pleasure seeking, imitation and repetition.

Dominant Center. At the level of processing information, one center takes the lead and this is the dominant center. Its values dominate the process of making sense out of life.

Enneagram of Personality. This is a system of nine personality types that uses the Pythagorean seal of a nine-pointed star in a circle with each type arranged clockwise around it. Each of the nine types is founded on the unconscious motivation of one of nine compulsions or passions: anger for the One, pride for the Two, deceit for the Three, envy for the Four, greed for the Five, fear for the Six, gluttony for the Seven, lust for the Eight, and sloth for the Nine. In Breakthrough Enneagram, these nine compulsions result from the way the three centers of intelligence are configured for that type. The way they interrelate creates a formula for the passion. Thus, from this perspective, moving from compulsion to freedom begins by untangling the three centers and developing each for its true purpose. Thus, the Enneagram is a nine-pointed system of false personality types. Each type is its own amalgamation of defense mechanisms united to protect a core misconception about oneself. Ones are the Achievers, who falsely believe they must live life perfectly to be loved. Twos, the Helpers, falsely believe they must give to others without restraint to be okay. Threes are the Succeeders, who falsely believe they must earn a place for themselves in the world through hard work and completing tasks. Fours are the Individualists; they falsely believe they earn the right to be loved by being authentic, deeply feeling people. Fives are the Observers, whose detached attitude leads to the false belief that enough objective information will fill the inner void and result in feeling safe in the world. Sixes, the Guardians, are traditionalists, the most domestic of all the types, who falsely believe they earn love by being responsible. Sevens, the Dreamers, are known for humor and their creative minds through which they falsely believe they earn love by making others happy. Eights are the Confronters; they falsely believe they are safe by being the most obviously powerful and controlling of all the types. Nines, the Preservationists, falsely believe that peace at any price brings them happiness. Different Enneagram theorists may use different labels or keywords for each of the nine types; however, they are all based on people's automatic responses and the false images they have of themselves.

False Personality. This is the most exterior part of the person. It is the home of the Enneagram compulsion. It is asleep and has no real will or real sense of self. However, by directing people's actions from unconsciousness, they are in a sleepwalking state, although they think they are conscious and awake.

Feeling Center. The purpose of the feeling center is to connect people both to their own souls and to realities outside themselves. The most helpful functions of this center include conscience and artistic creation, but when people are caught in their Enneagram compulsion it operates mostly in the realm of attentiveness to daily desires, emotional reactions, and personal likes and dislikes.

First Steps in Soul Development. In this book, the core of each Enneagram type is described through a unique configuration of the three centers of intelligence. By seeing how the centers are tangled with each other, the first steps to transformation or undoing your compulsion are clear: separate the dominant and support center and cultivate the true purposes of each, then develop the repressed center, making its gifts accessible.

Forgotten Child. When a center of intelligence is repressed, its growth is arrested in the childhood years. Thus, the child-like qualities associated with that center are lost and forgotten. Reclaiming these aspects of the "inner child" opens horizons of possibilities on the journey of transformation. The inner child of the thinking center is the bright, curious, questioning child lost to the dependent types (the three types who repress the thinking center — One, Two and Six). The feeling center's inner child is the spiritual, loving, gentle child forgotten by the aggressive types (the three types who repress this center — Three, Seven and Eight). The withdrawing types (the three types who repress the doing center — Four, Five and Nine) have lost touch with the adventuresome, spontaneous, playful child.

Formula for the Passion. The passions or compulsions are the core of each Enneagram type. The passion is formed from each type's unique configuration of centers, thus accounting for why each passion is associated with a particular type and not with others.

Levels of Consciousness. Consciousness is the state of awareness of the human mind. There are four levels or stages of human consciousness. The first is sleeping. The second is subjective consciousness (what people call "normal waking consciousness," and what the Enneagram of personality calls living in compulsion). The third is the state of Self-remembering. Objective consciousness is the fourth stage of consciousness.

My Best Self: Using the Enneagram to Free the Soul. This is Hurley and Donson's second book on the Enneagram of personality (Harper San Francisco, 1993). For the first time in Enneagram literature, it noted the fundamental relationship between the three centers of intelligence and the nine types. By showing each type as a unique configuration of centers, this book is the first presentation of the Enneagram to explain why there are nine and only nine Enneagram types. Incorporating major themes from Jungian psychology and from Gurdjieff's Work, it is the first book to relate these systems to the Enneagram.

Objective Consciousness. The end result of the transformation process is the ability to see things and people as they really are, including oneself. We attain objective consciousness because we have penetrated the veil of illusion of subjectivity the three centers of intelligence create when they are entwined with each other and egocentrically looking at themselves. Having been disengaged from each other to attain their true purposes, they can perceive the being of things. This ability is accompanied by a sense of bliss or release.

Opinions. An opinion is an idea a person learned from an outside source and has never questioned, or it is a prior thought that a person has never reexamined. When a person receives new information and thinks the issue through for him- or herself, either the opinion is discarded because it is invalid or the idea is internalized and validated, thus becoming a conviction.

Orientation to Time. As a way of masquerading the wound and repressed virtue, each Enneagram type develops an orientation to one of three aspects of time. Aggressive types are oriented to the future; their repressed virtue is love; thus, they don't have to love what doesn't yet exist. Dependent types are oriented to the immediate; their repressed virtue is faith; they don't need trust when dealing with reality directly present. Withdrawing types are oriented to the past; their repressed virtue is hope; thus, they don't need hope for things already completed.

Passion. The passion is the foundation of each of the nine types in the Enneagram of personality. The passion for the One is anger, for the Two is pride, for the Three is deceit, for the Four is envy, for the Five is greed, for the Six is fear, for the Seven is gluttony, for the Eight is lust, and for the Nine is sloth. This list of passions, with different wording at some points, comes from the writings of the desert Christian mystics (first to fifth century C. E.). Enneagram literature often refers to them as "compulsions." Breakthrough Enneagram views the compulsion or passion as *created* by a unique configuration of centers. The ranked order of preference of the centers is the formula for the passion and each type, because a type by definition has only one configuration of centers. There are only nine possible ways the three centers of intelligence (thinking, feeling, and doing) can interrelate. This is the foundation for the nine types of the Enneagram. The passion is an unconscious motivation created by the entanglement of the three centers. In this state, they draw forth from each other limited and patterned qualities that create a particular perspective on life that can be clearly seen through the nine Enneagram personality types. The centers are not meant to relate with each other in a self-hypnotic dance of mechanical activity; rather, they are mediators that should connect a person's true self or soul with others, the universe and Source. To reach this goal, the centers must be disentangled and each one developed independently to achieve its true purpose.

Personality. To engage with the world, human beings have to create an exterior expression of their soul, and this is called personality.

Potential Obstacles. Every type has a "down side" or blind spots due to the way the three centers of intelligence in that type are tangled and confused. Knowing these obstacles supports people of each type in recognizing them with clarity and dealing with them directly.

Preferred Center. In the Enneagram of personality, each of the nine types interprets the world through the values of one of the three centers of intelligence, which is called the preferred center. Twos, Threes and Fours see life through values of the feeling center such as personal likes and dislikes and projecting a favorable image. Fives, Sixes and Sevens view life through values of the thinking center such as the importance of information, analysis and depersonalizing situations. Eights, Nines and Ones approach life through the values of the doing center such as safety and energy output. The preferred center functions both as a lens that focuses people's attention on certain issues and as blinders that block out the importance of the issues the other two centers recognize. The overused preferred center tries to accomplish more than it was meant to accomplish. Through the overuse of a center, many strengths and talents develop. At the same time, many superficial and destructive qualities grow and dominate the false personality.

Qabalah. This body of wisdom is the Hebrew mystical or esoteric tradition. The word Qabalah means both "to reveal" (referring to explaining the inner nature of human beings) and "to receive" (referring to people's ability to receive inner wisdom and understanding). It is not an inner tradition only; the Qabalah teaches that no insight or inner experience has value unless it is grounded in daily life and the physical world.

Repressed Center. In the configuration of centers that creates the nine compulsions in the Enneagram of personality, the repressed center is in last place. Saying this center is repressed is *not* to say it is completely shut down or isn't present. Rather, this center is the least developed, having been left behind in the person's development, and therefore operates with immature values. This has happened because this center was wounded early in life, so its gifts have not been explored. Rather, these gifts are the object of mistrust and fear. Thus, this center is relegated to the unconscious. From there, it silently rules in the way an undisciplined and ignored child can rule a family: by disrupting it. Healthy development of the repressed center becomes a person's lifelong challenge and privilege. It is the heart of the process of transformation for each Enneagram type.

Repressed Virtue. As a result of the core wound, each of the types finds it difficult to express one of the three classical virtues needed for healing — faith, hope and love. The dependent types (Ones, Twos and Sixes) repress faith or trust and therefore focus their attention on the immediate situation. The aggressive types (Threes, Sevens and Eights) repress love and therefore find it difficult to pay attention to relationships without an ulterior motive. They also find it difficult to embrace feelings in others or themselves. As a result, they focus on the future. The withdrawing types (Fours, Fives and Nines) repress hope or the ability to welcome surprise in the material world, and thus they focus on the past.

Silent Witness. This aspect of one's inner self studies oneself objectively without self-condemnation or self-justification. The Silent Witness makes no commentary. It is best compared to turning on a light in a darkened room, then seeing and recording what is there. Sometimes called self-observation, this act's purpose is to recognize inner states. Using the Silent Witness part of them, people examine their motivations, explore which thoughts and feelings connect with each other and what behaviors they lead to. This process is usually a long one because people resist using their energy for inner work and taking responsibility for what goes on inside them. Through the Silent Witness process, spiritual seekers learn to admit who they really are and what they are really like without criticizing, justifying, rationalizing or condemning. Sometimes called the Inner Observer, Observing I, or the Observing Ego, this inner ability is foundational to all mystical spiritualities found both in the East and the West. It is also a prominent idea in modern psychology.

Soul. This is a traditional term often used to describe the nonmaterial aspect of human nature that engages with the world. It is an expression of spirit. Soul needs to be developed as a bridge between the material and nonmaterial realms. Other comparable terms are true self, real self and personhood.

Spirit. Not capitalized, this word refers to the most pure aspect of the nonmaterial part of human nature, the part of oneself that is contacted when meditation pierces through the layer of soul to an experience of self that is most authentically real. Another name for it is Essence. Capitalized, this word refers to the Uncreated (Source or God) from whom universal principles flow.

Spirituality. This is an inner movement by which human beings discover their spiritual nature, explore the world of soul, and learn to live from their true self instead of from their false personality or Enneagram compulsion.

Source. This is a name for the Uncreated (Spirit or God), from whom universal principles flow.

Support Center. In the configuration of centers that creates the nine compulsions in the Enneagram of personality, the support center falls in second place. Its energy serves the dominant center. This means the support center is not being used freely by the person. For example, two types have a support feeling center, One and Five. In Ones, the feeling center is devoted to the doing center, meaning they have many feelings about what they do, but there is little feeling energy left for relationships. In Fives, the support feeling center is devoted to ideas and, similarly, little feeling energy is left for relationships. The dominant center and support center create a team and settle into a patterned rhythm. They draw from each other both limited and predictable qualities that not only give rise to many strengths but also result in many weaknesses that dominate the false personality.

Thinking Center. The purpose of the intellectual or thinking center is to discriminate. The most helpful functions of this center include creative thought and initiating new ideas. But when people are caught in their Enneagram compulsion, the thinking center operates mostly in the realm of information, opinions, analysis and information gathering.

Three Centers of Intelligence. Foundational to the Enneagram is appreciation of the human person as a three-brained being. This idea of three intelligences creating the human mind is rooted in Greek philosophy from Plato on, as well as in the religious traditions of both East and West. In the modern era, it has been confirmed by science. Current research has discovered the human brain actually consists of three separate and distinct (though interconnected) layers. Each is considered to be the "home" of one of the three centers. They are called the three centers *of intelligence* because they are three aspects of the human mind. The process of maturation on the psychological level involves learning how to use these intelligences to survive and deal with the cares and anxieties of life. In this way, they form the passion that unconsciously drives people's lives. The passion makes them believe the illusion that they are living true to themselves when indeed they are spiritually asleep. The spiritual process of transformation involves disentangling the three centers and developing each one independently to achieve its true purpose.

Transformation. This is the process of inner work by which a person opens him- or herself to higher levels of consciousness to achieve objective consciousness (also called mystical union with the divine and self-realization). The Enneagram of personality can be the first step on the road to consciousness when the nine Enneagram types are seen as nine different configurations of the three centers of intelligence — thinking, feeling and doing. Using the Enneagram as a guide, people pursue transformation by balancing through inclusion. The process of transformation leads a person from living in false personality to rediscovering the true self.

Violence. Violence is any lack of respect for self or another. Examples are prejudice, answer giving, superiority, condescension, playing victim, manipulation and all negative emotions. There is also physical violence and war. Violence comes from the negative side of the feeling center and it can destroy what has awakened in human beings. Thus, the more people are negative, the less they understand and the more violent they become.

What's My Type? Use the Enneagram System of Nine Personality Types to Discover Your Best Self. This is Hurley and Donson's first book on the Enneagram of personality (Harper San Francisco, 1992). It focuses on the process of transformation for each of the Enneagram types and shows what people can do to overcome the limitations of their Enneagram type. It also was the first Enneagram book to incorporate the wisdom of the Qabalah for a deeper understanding of the spiritual core of each of the types.

Withdrawing Stance. Three types repress the doing center; they are the Four, Five and Nine. They withdraw in the sense that, deprived of the intelligence that connects them to the physical world and give them power to affect that world and get what they need, they look inside for ways to survive.

Wound. A person's Enneagram compulsion is formed by an early childhood wound to one of the three centers of intelligence. Betrayal is the wound to the thinking center, alienation/emotional isolation is the wound to the feeling center, and abandonment is the wound to the doing center. The wound causes that center to be repressed, and the repressed center is then in silent control of the false personality.

INDEX

Index notes: page references in italics indicate a figure; page references in bold indicate an entry in the Glossary; when entries are listed for each type, the types are arranged numerically, not alphabetically.

202–203, **234**
dependent stance, 33–34,
177–183, **237**
discovering types, 45–47
divine images of, 38,
237–238
dominant-support center
teams, 32–34, **238,
248–249**
false personalities, 20–22,
24, **240**
First Steps in Soul
Development, **240**
in the present moment,
175–192
learning and loving of,
195–196
nine types of personality,
34–39, 41–174
passions in types,
216–228, **243–244**
personality types, 13–16,
34–39, 41–174, **244**
potential obstacles, **244**
preferred center, 28–30,
245
repressed center of,
30–32, 176–192
role of, 43–47
Silent Witness of,
197–199
spirit, **248**

spiritual vitality, 12–16,
211–232
two-center intelligence,
31–34
withdrawing stance,
33–34, 177–178,
187–192, 218, **251**
wounding process, 24–27,
211–228
*Enneagram System of Nine
Personality Types to
Discover Your Best Self,*
38–39

F

false personality, 20–22, 24,
240
See also specific type
feeling center of intelligence, 15, 20–22,
204–205, 217, **240**
first steps in soul development, **240**
for the One, 52–53
for the Two, 66–67
for the Three, 80–81
for the Four, 94–95
for the Five, 108–09
for the Six, 122–23
for the Seven, 136–37
for the Eight, 150–51

The Authors

Kathy Hurley and Theodorre Donson are authors of three books, pioneers in the spirituality of the Enneagram, gifted speakers and seminar presenters, consultants, and leaders in the international Enneagram community. Having researched many different spiritual and psychological disciplines for over 30 years each, they have created a practical, profound yet simple system for healing the human soul; it uses understanding of one's Enneagram type as a guide and mirror on the journey. Their training programs have attracted therapists, human resources personnel, clergy and other leaders in the field of personal growth from all over the world. Their passion is personal and societal change through non-violent inner work.

Contact the Authors

Enneagram Resources, Inc.
12262 W. New Mexico Ave.
Lakewood, Colorado 80228
U. S. A.

Phone: 303.985.1889
Toll Free: 877.591.9903
E-mail:ERI@hurleydonson.com
Website: www.hurleydonson.com

Services

ENNEAGRAM TRAINING AND
CERTIFICATION PROGRAMS
*Five-day programs for
individual personal growth and
certification to teach the Enneagram*
<u>Topics include:</u>
Principles for discovering
the true self and dissolving the
Enneagram compulsion
Recognizing type in self and others
Working with centers for healing
Teaching the Enneagram as a path
to liberation and wholeness
*Consult the web site and/or
Call toll free for more information*

BOOKS, AUDIO CASSETTES
AND OTHER PRODUCTS
*Call our office toll free
or visit our on-line store
at our web site*

SEMINARS AND RETREATS
Discover Your Soul Potential
Breakthrough Enneagram®
Nine Pathways to the Soul
Enneagram for Team Building
Steps to Dissolving Violence in
Relationships, Families and
Communities
*Call toll free for details about
individualized topics, formats
and fees*

INDIVIDUAL TYPING SESSIONS,
CONSULTATION AND
SPIRITUAL DIRECTION
*In person or by phone
For appointments and fees*
Contact Kathy directly at
303.985.1889
Contact Theodorre directly at
303.980.8141

Distributed to the trade by
BLESSINGWAY BOOKS, INC.
P. O. Box 31280
Santa Fe, New Mexico 87594
Phone: 505.483.3700 • Fax: 505.438.3704
For orders only, call 800.716.2953
E-mail: blessingway@blessingway.com
Web site: www.blessingway.com

Publishing Consultation by
Christine Testolini
THE INTEGRITY AGENCY
Littleton, Colorado 80127
Phone: 303.933.6778 • Fax: 303.973.8647
E-mail:ctest@ecentral.com

A NOTE FROM THE AUTHORS

We greatly enjoy hearing from readers for whom our books have made a difference in their lives. Although we cannot respond personally, we will read your letter or e-mail. Also let us know if you want to be on our mailing list.

Kathy and Theodorre